UNDERSTANDING EMOTIONAL HEALING

Experiencing Freedom
by Changing Our Perception!

Steve Lapp & Jacob Lapp
Forward by Dr. Myles Munroe

Understanding Emotional Healing

Copyright © 2013 Steve Lapp and Jacob Lapp

UNDERSTANDING EMOTIONAL HEALING
47 Common Blocks to Healing Plus Many Secrets & Keys to Freedom!

Printed in the USA

ISBN: 978-0-9995776-0-8

Library of Congress Control Number: 2014947632

All Rights Reserved. This book is protected by the copyright laws of the United States of America. This book may not be copied or reprinted for commercial gain or profit. The use of short quotations is permitted. Permission will be granted upon request. The author guarantees all contents are original and do not infringe upon the legal rights of any other person or work.

To contact the author or reorder:

Impact Media Publishing, LLC
P.O. Box 567
Ephrata, PA 17522
(717)696-5418
sales@impactmediapublishing.com
www.lappbrothers.com

All scripture references are KJV unless otherwise mentioned.

Understanding Emotional Healing

FOREWORD

"UNDERSTANDING EMOTIONAL HEALING" is an erudite, eloquent, and immensely thought-provoking work that gets to the heart of the deepest struggles and aspirations of the human heart and addresses the contemporary culture of despair and loneliness gripping our present generation.

UNDERSTANDING EMOTIONAL HEALING is indispensable reading for anyone who wants to understand how to overcome the mystery of spiritual and emotional healing in areas of our lives that we keep suppressed. This is a profound authoritative work which spans the wisdom of the ages and yet breaks new ground in its approach to understanding the modern man. This book will possibly become a classic in this and the next generation.

This exceptional work by Steve & Jacob Lapp is one of the most profound, practical, principle-centered approaches to this subject of True Emotional Healing I have read in a long time. The author's approach to this timely issue brings a fresh breath of air that captivates the heart, engages the mind and inspires the spirit of the reader.

The title of this book alone "UNDERSTANDING EMOTIONAL HEALING" should make it a must read for all humanity. The cultural hopelessness and disillusionment among the nations makes this book more valuable than ever. There is not a race,

Understanding Emotional Healing

culture, or group of people on the planet who are not being devastated by the attack on their emotional stability.

The author's ability to leap over complicated theological and metaphysical jargon and reduce complex theories to simple practical principles that the least among us can understand is amazing.

This work will challenge the intellectual while embracing the laymen as it dismantles the mysteries of the soul search of mankind and delivers the profound in simplicity.

Steve and Jacob's approach awakens in the reader the untapped inhibiters that retard our personal development and their antidotes empower us to rise above these self-defeating, self-limiting factors to a life of exploits in spiritual, mental and emotional advancement.

The authors also integrate into each chapter the time-tested precepts giving each principle a practical application to life making the entire process people-friendly.

UNDERSTANDING EMOTIONAL HEALING is pregnant with wisdom and powerful principles and I enjoyed the mind-expanding experience of this exciting work. I admonish you to plunge into this ocean of knowledge and watch your life change for the better.

Dr. Myles Munroe
BFM International
ITWLA
Nassau Bahamas

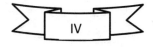

Understanding Emotional Healing

Special thanks to Elsie Lapp, Naomi King, and David Lapp for the work they contributed by editing, proofing, and producing this project.

Understanding Emotional Healing

We suggest you take notes, highlight, or simply write into your book as you read it.

Understanding Emotional Healing

CONTENTS

Chapter 1:
13 - What is Emotional Healing?
    14 - Things That Should Never Happen to Anyone
    16 - Things Often Withheld That Everyone Needs
    16 - Separating the Person from the Influence
    17 - Processing from the Heart Vs. The Mind

Chapter 2:
19 - Identity
    19 - Who Am I
    22 - Why Am I Here
    25 - Where Am I Going
    25 - Who Cares
    27 - What Is Your 'I Am'

Chapter 3:
29 - Identifying Ancient Strongholds
    30 - Generational Iniquities
    33 - Idolatry
    35 - Bloodshed
    37 - Broken Covenants
    40 - Sexual Immorality (Caused by Compromise)
    43 - Compromise

Chapter 4:
51 - Blocks to Healing (A-C)
    53 - Abandonment
    57 - Accusations
    58 - Addictions

Understanding Emotional Healing

    61 - Anger
    63 - Anxiety
    64 - Bitterness
    66 - Blame
    68 - Burnout
    69 - Comparisons
    70 - Condemnations
    72 - Control
    73 - Covetousness

Chapter 5:
75 - Blocks to Healing (D-H)
    75 - Death Wishes
    76 - Denial
    78 - Depression
    81 - Discouragement
    83 - Double-Mindedness
    84 - Envy
    86 - 'Fantasy World'
    87 - Fear
    93 - Gossip
    95 - Guilt
    97 - Hopelessness

Chapter 6:
101 - Blocks to Healing (I-R)
    101 - Insecurity
    102 - Insinuations
    104 - Jealousy
    105 - Judgments
    107 - Lust
    110 - Manipulation
    111 - Offenses
    112 - Performance
    114 - Pride
    117 - Rebellion
    119 - Rejection
    121 - Resentment
    123 - Retaliation

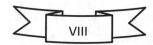

Understanding Emotional Healing

Chapter 7:
129 - Blocks to Healing (S-Z)
    129 - Self-Pity
    132 - Selfishness
    134 - Sex (Unholy)
    137 - Sex (Withheld)
    139 - Shame
    141 - Soul Ties
    143 - Stress
    144 - Unbelief
    146 - Unforgiveness
    148 - Victim Mentality
    151 - Vows, Oaths, and Agreements

Chapter 8:
153 - Keys to Overcoming
    153 - Acceptance
    155 - Authority
    157 - Forgiveness
    159 - Grace
    160 - Gratefulness
    162 - Joy of the Lord
    163 - Peace that Passes Understanding
    164 - Perfect Love Casts Out Fear
    166 - The Power of Our Words
    167 - The Power of Submission
    169 - The Power of the Trash Can
    171 - The Shelf
    172 - The Truth Will Make Us Free

Chapter 9:
175 - Steps to Overcoming
    176 - Repentance and Salvation
    178 - Activating Our Will and Taking Responsibility
    179 - Closing Doors
    180 - Taking Every Thought Captive
    181 - Feelings Buried Alive Never Die
    182 - Turn On the Light

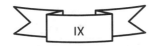

Understanding Emotional Healing

    183 - Trading
    184 - Healing Vs. Divine Health
    185 - Unity in Diversity
    187 - Laying Up Treasures in Heaven

Chapter 10:
189 - Process of Maturity
    190 - Memories
    192 - Triggers
    193 - Weaning
    195 - Maturity
    197 - Discipleship
    198 - Sonship
    200 - Community
    201 - Body of Christ

Chapter 11:
203 - How to Help People with Emotional Issues
    204 - The Position and Process
    205 - The Power of Asking Questions
    208 - The Ability to Listen
    210 - Changing Our Perceptions
    212 - Counseling Sessions Vs. Relationships

Chapter 12:
213 - Aligning the Spirit, Soul, and Body
    215 - Feeding the Spirit, Soul, and Body
    217 - Connecting to the Source
    218 - Being an Overcomer
    220 - Using the Owner's Manual

Understanding Emotional Healing

Understanding Emotional Healing is dedicated to everyone who is struggling with emotional issues.

It is also designed for the people who want to learn how to help people that are struggling with emotional issues, and anyone looking for more abundance in their life.

Understanding Emotional Healing is loaded with keys that explain why people do what they do, why they think the way they think, and why they act the way they act.

We purposely repeated a few specific points to emphasize them.

Understanding Emotional Healing

Chapter 1: What is Emotional Healing?

True emotional healing is seeing things from God's point of view, and allowing God to heal any wounds of the heart that are keeping us from trusting Him. To do this, we need to start where people are, not where we want them to be.

Emotional healing is taking an honest look at what is going on in a person's heart.
- What are the things that are happening to us that should never happen to anyone?
- What are the things that we are not receiving that everyone needs?
- How am I being influenced in my life?
- How can we process life from the heart rather than being stuck in the mind?
- Why is it important to engage our heart rather than just live from the mind?
- What are the unanswered questions that are going on in the heart?

Understanding Emotional Healing

Four basic areas to address in order for healing to happen:
- Sin needs to be repented of
- Lies need to be replaced with truth
- Demons need to be cast out
- Wounds need to be healed

Things That Should Never Happen to Anyone

Unfortunately many people suffer from abuse or pressure patterns in their life. Abuse can happen in many different ways. Some examples of abuse are:
- Physical abuse
- Emotional abuse
- Verbal abuse
- Psychological abuse
- Sexual abuse
- Spiritual abuse
- Spousal abuse

What is abuse? It is when a person in a relationship uses a pattern of behaviors to control the other person.

Abuse is when someone is:
- Pushing, hitting, slapping, choking, kicking, or biting
- Shaking, burning, pinching, throwing, or beating
- Inflicting actions that cause physical injury, leave marks, or cause pain
- Threatening you, your children, other family members, or pets
- Threatening suicide to get you to do something
- Using or threatening to use a weapon against you

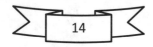

What is Emotional Healing?

- Using finances to manipulate and control
- Putting you down or making you feel bad
- Using guilt trips, humiliation, intimidation, or mind games
- Name-calling, making threats, or yelling
- Forcing you to have sex, or to do sexual acts that you do not want, like, understand, or that are wrong
- Keeping you from seeing your friends, family, or from going to work

Some people have trouble recognizing when they are being abused. A person might think that is just the way things are and that there's nothing that can be done.

Sometimes abusers will convince the person being abused that it is their fault that they are being abused. Sometimes abusers manipulate those that they are abusing by telling them that they did something wrong, or "asked for it".

Keeping the abuse a secret doesn't protect anyone from being abused – it only makes it more likely that the abuse will continue (to others if not to you.)

What are pressure patterns? It is the pressure that is put on someone to perform, in order to get the acceptance and affirmation that is needed for survival.

Most of us have not been loved according to who we are, but we've been loved according to what we can perform or do.

Understanding Emotional Healing

Things Often Withheld That Everyone Needs

Many people have never heard their father say, "I love you". Because of this, they may have a hard time trusting God. We were designed by God to receive love freely and to give it away. If this action is hindered in our lives, we will have a hard time trusting God, others, and even ourselves.

Every living person needs:
- Affirmation
- Attention
- Affection
- Love
- Acceptance
- Power
- Fun
- Freedom
- To belong

A person who can get his needs met directly from God will experience the ultimate freedom. Until this can happen, it is important for us to be able to supply this to our children, and to those who have been extremely hurt and traumatized when they were children.

Separating the Person from the Influence

Many people believe that there are three influences in our life. God's kingdom, the devil's kingdom, and ourselves.

What is Emotional Healing?

We believe there are only two influences[1], God's kingdom, and the devil's kingdom. We always come into agreement with one or the other of these two influences.

If the Spirit of God is working in us, we will be influenced by the Holy Spirit and will manifest good fruit[2].

If the enemy is working in us, we will be influenced by demonic forces and fleshly desires[3] and will manifest evil fruit.

We are created in God's image but we do things according to which spirit influences us.

Processing from the Heart Vs. the Mind

The heart processes information many times faster than the mind. However, many people have their heart shut down and are trying to figure life out from their brain. This can be the cause of much stress, confusion, and frustration, etc.

Our hearts are designed for relationship. It is impossible to have a relationship without engaging the heart. This is why it is so important to trust in the Lord with all our heart, and lean not on our own mind (understanding[4]).

---

[1] Matthew 7:20 Wherefore by their fruits ye shall know them.

[2] Galatians 5:22-23 But the fruit of the Spirit is love, joy, peace, long-suffering, gentleness, goodness, faith, Meekness, temperance: against such there is no law.

[3] Romans 1:29-31 Being filled with all unrighteousness, fornication, wickedness, covetousness, maliciousness; full of envy, murder, debate, deceit, malignity; whisperers, Backbiters, haters of God, despiteful, proud, boasters, inventors of evil things, disobedient to parents, Without understanding, covenant breakers, without natural affection, implacable, unmerciful:

[4] Proverbs 3:5 Trust in the LORD with all thine heart; and lean not unto thine own understanding.

Understanding Emotional Healing

Emotional pain is always caused by unanswered questions of the heart. These questions are usually connected to personal identity questions.

In order to open up the heart, it is necessary to be willing to take an honest look at the questions of the heart and to be willing to address any blockages or hindrances that prevent the flow of healing.

Remember, love opens up a heart[5], and the truth will make you free[6].

---

[5] 2 Thessalonians 3:5 And the Lord direct your hearts into the love of God, and into the patient waiting for Christ.

[6] John 8:32 And ye shall know the truth, and the truth shall make you free.

Chapter 2:
Identity

Every emotional issue is connected to an identity question. These are questions such as "Who am I?", "Why am I here?", "Where am I going?", and "Who cares?".

Our true identity is exactly who God says we are. The enemy comes in and tries to make us believe that we are something we are not. This causes a lot of problems and allows the enemy to put things on our lives, based on our own belief system in the wrong identity.

It is important to resolve these identity questions and to reconcile them with God.

Who Am I

We are who we are because of who God made us and what Jesus did, not because of what we can do. This is the reason we

Understanding Emotional Healing

are called human beings, and not human doings. If we get that in order, we don't have to worry about who we are. We can love each other for who God made us to be.

We are spiritual beings. We are invisible spiritual beings.

What you see here is not me, it is a vehicle that I get around in. It is my earth suit. When we go to space, we need a spacesuit. To live here on earth, we need an earth suit.

It is easy for us to get focused on the vehicle, instead of the person. We can get focused on how things look, or how people act, instead of who people are.

There are very few people who, as little children, were loved exactly for who they were. To really fully experience love, we have to experience love for who we are, not because of what we did or didn't do. We are loved because we were made in God's image. For example, God so loved the world... [7]

I am persuaded [8] that neither life, nor death, nor angels, nor principalities, nor powers, can separate us from the love of God.

If we are running from God, we can never run anywhere that He can't find us. We can love people, whether they want it or not. God is everywhere, and perfect love casts out all fear.

---

[7] John 3:16 For God so loved the world, that he gave his only begotten Son, that whosoever believeth in in him should not perish, but have everlasting life.

[8] Romans 8:38-39 For I am persuaded, that neither death, nor life, nor angels, nor principalities, nor powers, nor things present, nor things to come, Nor height, nor depth, nor any other creature, shall be able to separate us from the love of God, which is in Christ Jesus our Lord.

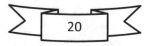

Identity

Perfect love is not only an experience, because it is actually a spirit. For God has not given us the spirit[9] of fear, but the Spirit of power, and of love, and of a sound mind.

The mental institutes are full of people who do not have a sound mind. The way we understand this is they have a spirit of fear.

We were working at a faith based program where people had to go through counseling to get evaluated before they could receive the free medication provided by this program.

A man came in to participate in the program. He was upset because we were in the room ready to counsel him, instead of the doctor that he was expecting.

We asked him a few questions, but he was not interested in being counseled. He only wanted to see a psychiatrist and receive his medications. He tried to intimidate us by saying, "Don't ask me questions. It makes me want to kill somebody."

We knew that if someone is angry, they are fearful, and perfect love will cast out all fear. Anger is always an attempt to keep others away from our pain.

This guy actually looked like he wanted to kill somebody. We asked him, "What is your fear? What are you afraid of?"

He emphatically said, "I'm not afraid of anything."

---

[9] 2 Timothy 1:7 For God hath not given us the spirit of fear; but of power, and of love, and of a sound mind.

Understanding Emotional Healing

We knew by him saying, "I'm not afraid of anything," he turned the valve off to his fear.

Then we asked him, "Why won't you answer our questions?"

He said, "I'll answer your questions."

We were then able to talk with him, and connect with his heart, and within a few minutes he connected to his own heart and started to cry. He was set free that day. In a matter of a few minutes, he went from wanting to kill us, to crying.

A few weeks later we met him again and he was a completely different person.

The secret to setting him free was to get him to connect with his heart and identify his agreements with the enemy.

We then got him to break his agreements with the enemy, and to come into agreement with God, and be willing to do things God's way.

Jesus died on the cross so that the whole world could be saved. Our mission on earth is to help people to break their agreements with the devil, help them to receive what Jesus died and paid for, help them to trust God, come into agreement with Him, and live their life according to God's plan for them.

Why Am I Here

Our general purpose in life is to establish the Kingdom of God here on earth, and to influence earth with the culture of Heaven.

Identity

We are to do this by displaying the fruit[10] of the Spirit, and by demonstrating the gifts[11] of the Spirit.

God wants to express his glory here on earth. He put us in these earth suits (human bodies), so that when we submit, He can manifest Himself through us and magnify His glory.

When the disciples asked Jesus to teach them how to pray, he showed them the heart and the purpose of the Father. He taught them to pray for the Father's Kingdom to come, and the Father's will to be done, in earth[12] (in us) exactly the same as it is in Heaven.

If God's Kingdom is to be manifested here on earth as it is in Heaven, that means we need access to His Character and to His Spirit. Jesus came to give us access. He said, "I am the Way, the Truth, and the Life[13]." That means we can be fully alive and live at our full potential here on earth.

On everyone's tombstone there is a dash (-) between the date they were born, and the date they died. It does not matter how many years they were alive, the dash (-) is the same size.

---

[10] Galatians 5:22-23 But the fruit of the Spirit is love, joy, peace, long-suffering, gentleness, goodness, faith, Meekness, temperance: against such there is no law.

[11] 1 Corinthians 12:8-10 For to one is given by the Spirit the word of wisdom; to another the word of knowledge by the same Spirit; To another faith by the same Spirit; to another the gifts of healing by the same Spirit; To another the working of miracles; to another prophecy; to another discerning of spirits; to another divers kinds of tongues; to another the interpretation of tongues:

[12] Matthew 6:10 Thy kingdom come. Thy will be done in earth, as it is in heaven.

[13] John 14:6 Jesus saith unto him, I am the way, the truth, and the life: no man cometh unto the Father, but by me.

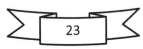

Understanding Emotional Healing

The dash (-) is the determining factor of what was accomplished in someone's lifetime. God has a plan for everyone here on the earth, and we have the time between birth and death to accomplish God's plan and purpose for our life.

If we don't accomplish the plans and purposes that God has for our life, in the dash (-) of time that we have here on earth, then it will not get done by anybody.

We are called to do specific things, and every person has a unique Godly purpose and plan. Are we going to fulfill that purpose and plan, or will it be unfulfilled when we go to our grave?

The graveyards have a lot of unfulfilled purpose that people took with them to the grave when they died, instead of releasing their God given gift to the world.

We are here to represent God's people. God is interested in a group of people working together as one. We are to represent God to the world and to other Christians.

In the same way the Father (God) sent Jesus into the world, Jesus is now sending[14] us into the world to represent the Father. We are to represent Father God to everyone we meet, so that the world may know that the Father has sent Jesus, and has loved us the very same way[15] that He loved Jesus.

---

[14] John 20:21 Then said Jesus to them again, Peace be unto you: as my Father has sent me, even so send I you.

[15] John 17:23 I in them, and thou in me, that they may be made perfect in one; and that the world may know that thou hast sent me, and hast loved them, as thou hast loved me.

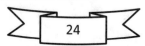

Identity

Where Am I Going

Many people have this question, "Where am I going?"

Jesus said, "Go ye into all the world[16]..." He also said, "Go ye therefore, and teach all nations[17]..."

He did not say, "Sit ye in a pew..."

Jesus went to prepare a place for us in His Father's house. When He is ready for us there, He will come to receive[18] us to be with Him.

The purpose of becoming a follower of Jesus is not to go to Heaven. The purpose is to take back ground from the enemy, and re-establish the Kingdom of God while we are still living on earth.

Who Cares

Many people are asking the question, is there anyone who cares about me? Does anyone understand what I struggle with or what I am going through?

Jesus cares about every person and so should His body. If we

---

[16] Mark 16:15 And he said unto them, Go ye into all the world, and preach the gospel to every creature.

[17] Matthew 28:19-20 Go ye therefore, and teach all nations, baptizing them in the name of the Father, and of the Son, and of the Holy Ghost: Teaching them to observe all things whatsoever I have commanded you: and, lo, I am with you alway, even unto the end of the world. Amen.

[18] John 14:2-3 In my Father's house are many mansions: if it were not so, I would have told you. I go to prepare a place for you. And if I go and prepare a place for you, I will come again, and receive you unto myself; that where I am, there ye may be also.

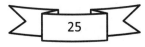

Understanding Emotional Healing

do not care about each other, then how can we be representing Jesus' true body?

There is a big difference between caring about a person's heart, or in accepting their behavior and deeds.

As we go through life we get fed in three different realms. In the spiritual realm, in the soul realm, and in the physical realm.

In the physical realm we get fed by the food that we eat.

How do we get fed in the spirit realm? By the Word of God? By reading the Bible? By prayer? Actually, our spirit gets fed by revelation. For example, the revelation of the Word of God, by the Holy Spirit making Truth real to our life.

It is possible to read the Bible without getting any revelation or inspiration. However, when this happens, our spirit is not getting fed. Only when we get a revelation can our spirit be fed by the written Word.

How does our soul get fed? Our soul gets fed by acceptance.

For example, a couple might be living in sin and decide to go to church one Sunday morning.

When they get to the church building, they are not wearing the right clothes, they might sit in the wrong pew, and they might not act the right way. They do not feel acceptance from the people and leave discouraged.

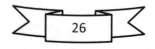

Identity

They then go down to the local bar, and as they enter they are welcomed in by the people. Who fed their soul that day? Who gave them acceptance? Could it be that the local bar is providing a false acceptance instead of the church providing a true acceptance?

What would happen if Christians would do a better job of accepting each other, and non-Christians, without accepting wrong behaviors and sin?

If this would happen, we would be able to help people get rid of their wrong behaviors and sin, and help them get right with God.

What Is Your 'I Am'

Your 'I am' is the belief system that your heart and mind operate by.

Some people have an 'I am' that says:
- I am worthless
- I am stupid
- I am lazy
- I am hopeless
- I am a failure
- I am trash
- I am dirty
- I am a nuisance
- I am...

This type of 'I am' will keep us from connecting to God, and the promises of God.

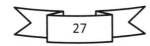

Understanding Emotional Healing

When we become born again and adopted into God's Kingdom, then our 'I am' will change. Now it becomes:
- I am a child of God[19]
- I am seated with Christ in the heavenly realm[20]
- I am adopted[21] into God's family
- I am forgiven
- I am the light of the world[22]
- I am accepted
- I am blessed
- I am an overcomer
- I am more than a conqueror
- I am...

When our 'I am' is in agreement with God, we will be able to overcome[23] the enemy.

However, many people struggle with two programs running at the same time. Part of them is in agreement with God, and part of them is in agreement with the enemy. This causes double-mindedness.

---

[19] Galatians 3:26 For ye are all the children of God by faith in Christ Jesus.

[20] Ephesians 2:6 And has raised us up together, and made us sit together in heavenly places in Christ Jesus:

[21] Romans 8:15 For ye have not received the spirit of bondage again to fear; but ye have received the Spirit of adoption, whereby we cry, Abba, Father.

[22] Matthew 5:14 Ye are the light of the world. A city that is set on an hill cannot be hid.

[23] Philippians 4:13 I can do all things through Christ which strengtheneth me.

Chapter 3:
Identifying Ancient Strongholds

Stronghold is a military term. It is a portion of territory that refuses to submit to the ruling authority.

A stronghold is an area of darkness, often within our mind or personality, that causes ongoing spiritual, emotional, and/or behavioral problems. It is the fruit of an inward lie.

A stronghold is a faulty thinking pattern based on lies and deception. Deception is one of the primary weapons of the devil, because it is the building blocks for a stronghold.

With our permission, a lie can gain control over our emotions and our behavior which creates a stronghold.

A stronghold can be any mindset that is contrary to God's Word. If a person has an inner pulling toward a sin and moves towards it, it can become a stronghold.

Understanding Emotional Healing

People who suffer serious emotional trauma are prime candidates for spiritual strongholds. Ongoing memories of painful events prepare the heart to accept the suggestions, lies, and influence of darkness.

If we are preoccupied with our painful past then we will not be able to live out the redemptive victories of Jesus Christ. We will not be able to grow in faith and we will not be able to possess our new identity in Christ or walk it out.

Painful memories can and will drive us to bitterness, hatred, anxiety, or depression, but the Word of God will bring us healing.

Even when we forgive the person or people that have hurt us, if the painful memories continue to recycle, then we can remain under the influence of those painful memories.

Strongholds are usually mental in nature, but they affect every part of our being. Feeling our feelings frees us to re-examine our ideas and to correct the ones that aren't right. This will tear down the strongholds.

Other causes of strongholds can be generational iniquities, idolatry, bloodshed, broken covenants, and sexual immorality, etc.

Generational Iniquities

Many people are plagued with things that were passed down through the generations by their forefathers. These things often become a stumbling block or even a stronghold in the family tree.

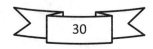

Identifying Ancient Strongholds

Many people do not like to look at this aspect of their lives because they don't want to take responsibility for their forefathers' sins.

However, when we begin to see the benefits of breaking these sin patterns and the sin cycles in our family tree, then we can see this in an entirely different light.

We can get excited that God has made a way, not only for us and our children, but also for our entire family tree to experience freedom.

An iniquity is a sin pattern that is committed over and over again, such as:
- Getting drunk time and time again
- Committing adultery again and again
- Stealing
- Gossip
- Lying
- Taking drugs
- Etc.

These sin patterns tend to repeat themselves in the following generations if they are not dealt with.

When we first heard about generational curses and iniquities, we talked about an issue that we brothers and sisters struggled with. We realized that our mother and our grandmother also struggled with the same thing.

We decided to pray, confess, and repent for this issue on a generational level.

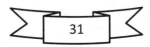

Understanding Emotional Healing

When we finished praying, our children, who were sleeping in three different rooms in the house, immediately woke up and started vomiting and then went right back to sleep.

Even though we had a mess to clean up it was exciting, because it was confirmed to us that what we had just prayed about and experienced was real.

Later on a couple told us that they were able to have only one child. The wife also had cousins who either had no children or only one child. One of her cousins had gone to the doctor to find out what the problem was. The doctor told her that it was a genetic defect in their family that was causing this.

We realized that this was a generational curse that was at work in their family tree. We helped her to pray through, take authority over, and destroy the generational curse.

Soon after this she became pregnant. What was really exciting was that two of her cousins, who didn't even know about the prayers that were prayed, became pregnant too.

The Bible talks about generational curses and iniquities being passed on to three or four generations. It also talks about generational blessings being passed on to a thousand generations.

What a blessing when we can get rid of the generational curses and iniquities that were blocking the flow in our lives, and we can begin to experience the generational blessings the way God designed them to be experienced!

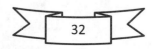

Identifying Ancient Strongholds

<u>Example prayer:</u>

Lord, I want to do like Daniel did in Daniel chapter 9. I take responsibility and repent for my sins, the sins of my forefathers, and the sins of my people.

Lord, I stand in the gap and repent for the generational sins of _____ (name the sin) _____ and I bring it all to You at the cross.

Lord, I ask that you would apply the blood of Jesus to these iniquities, and cleanse my entire family tree from all unrighteousness connected to these sins.

And Lord, I ask that you would release the generational blessings that were held back by these curses.

In Jesus Name, Amen.

Idolatry

Idolatry is the human tendency to value something or someone, in a way that hinders the love and trust we owe to God.

Idolatry is an act of theft from God, whereby we use some part of creation, in a way that steals from the honor due to God.

Whatever we worship, we will serve. Worship and service are always intimately bound together. We enter into covenant service with whatever most captures our imagination and heart.

Understanding Emotional Healing

If we worship anything other than God, it will ensnare us into idolatry.

Many churches today have more interest in following the traditions[24], the methods, and the practices of the leaders before them, than they do of seeking God's will and purposes for their church today.

They have a form of godliness, but they deny God's power[25]. This is a form of idolatry that conflicts with our putting God first in our lives, and in what we love and trust.

The Bible reveals to us that even stubbornness[26] and the praise of men[27] is considered as idolatry.

Example prayer:

Lord, I take responsibility and repent for the sins of idolatry. I take responsibility and repent for my sins, the sins of my forefathers, and the sins of my people.

Lord, I repent on behalf of the church for following the traditions of man instead of seeking God's will and purposes for the church.

---

[24] Mark 7:9 And he said unto them, Full well ye reject the commandment of God, that ye may keep your own tradition.

[25] 2 Timothy 3:5 Having a form of godliness, but denying the power thereof: from such turn away.

[26] 1 Samuel 15:23 For rebellion is as the sin of witchcraft, and stubbornness is as iniquity and idolatry. Because thou hath rejected the word of the LORD, he hath also rejected thee from being king.

[27] John 12:43 For they loved the praise of men more than the praise of God.

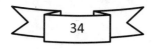

Identifying Ancient Strongholds

Lord, I ask that You would apply the blood of Jesus to these sins, and cleanse us from all unrighteousness connected to these sins.

I choose to humble myself to You, Lord, and to worship only You.

In Jesus Name, Amen.

Bloodshed

Bloodshed is the destruction of life, as in war or murder. It especially pertains to loss of life on a large scale.

In Germany, the Jews were slaughtered by Hitler. The natural explanation is that it happened because Hitler hated the Jews.

However, in the spirit realm it is obvious that the devil wanted the Jews eradicated from the earth because they are God's chosen people[28].

In America, there was a lot of bloodshed, especially of the Native Americans. This bloodshed causes a curse to come upon the land and upon the nation. The blood cries[29] out to God for justice.

---

[28] Acts 3:25 Ye are the children of the prophets, and of the covenant which God made with our fathers, saying unto Abraham, And in thy seed shall all the kindreds of the earth be blessed.

[29] Genesis 4:10 And he said, What has thou done? the voice of thy brother's blood crieth unto me from the ground. And now art thou cursed from the earth, which hath opened her mouth to receive thy brother's blood from thy hand;

Understanding Emotional Healing

Also there is a lot of innocent blood that is shed in the form of abortion. This is an abomination that allows a curse to come upon the nation and upon the people, especially the people directly involved.

We had a conversation with a person who had been involved in the occult world but had come out of it.

He told us that when abortion became legal in America the demonic forces had so much extra energy released that they did not know what to do with it all.

He confirmed that they knew in the demonic realm that this was a sacrifice to Molech[30].

Example prayer:

Lord, I take responsibility and repent for my sins, the sins of my forefathers, the sins of my people, and the sins of our nation, for rejecting God's chosen people, the Jews.

Lord, I also repent for the bloodshed of the Native Americans and of the atrocities of wars that caused the spilling of blood and the loss of life.

Lord, I realize that this includes the bloodshed of abortions that has been legalized in America. I repent for allowing abortions to be legal in America.

---

[30] Leviticus 18:21 And thou shalt not let any of thy seed pass through the fire to Molech, neither shalt thou profane the name of thy God: I am the LORD.

Identifying Ancient Strongholds

I ask, Lord, that you would break and destroy the curse of these sins, and also break and destroy any allegiance to the devil and to Molech.

Lord, I ask for the blood of Jesus to cleanse us from these iniquities and to restore us to purity and righteousness.

In Jesus Name, Amen.

Broken Covenants

A covenant is an agreement between two people, a treaty between nations, or a relationship between God and a human individual or nation. A covenant involves loyalty and allegiance, not just a financial exchange.

A covenant is not just something that we can agree to and then break it whenever it's inconvenient to keep it.

A covenant is a binding agreement between two parties that each party will keep even if it is not popular to do so.

The Bible tells us that God made an everlasting covenant with Abraham's seed.

Many churches today have chosen to break this everlasting covenant[31], and have chosen to believe that the Jews are no longer God's chosen people.

---

[31] Genesis 17:5-7 Neither shall thy name any more be called Abram, but thy name shall be Abraham; for a father of many nations have I made thee. And I will make thee exceeding fruitful, and I will make nations of thee, and kings shall come out of thee. And I will establish my covenant between me and thee and thy seed after thee in their generations for an everlasting covenant, to be a God unto thee, and to thy seed after thee.

Understanding Emotional Healing

If it was true that the Jews are no longer God's chosen people, then it could not have been an everlasting covenant.

These broken covenants bring consequences[32] upon the church, such as:
- Church splits
- Religious strongholds
- Spiritually dead churches
- Sexual immorality
- Divorce
- Etc.

The American government has made many covenants with the Native Americans throughout the years.

These covenants have been broken over and over and over again by the government. These broken covenants have a lasting, even generational, negative effect on Americans today.

One of the negative results of these broken covenants is an ongoing curse upon people, coming together in agreement in marriage, but ending up in divorce (broken covenant) when things don't go their way.

Broken covenants cause hearts to harden. And hardness[33] of the heart causes broken covenants.

---

[32] Ezekiel 17:19 Therefore thus saith the Lord GOD; As I live, surely mine oath that he hath despised, and my covenant that he hath broken, even it will I recompense upon his own head.

[33] Matthew 19:8 He said unto them, Moses because of the hardness of your hearts suffered you to put away your wives: but from the beginning it was not so.

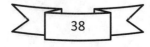

Identifying Ancient Strongholds

If we do not walk according to God's plans and purposes, we will see splits and divisions in any group of people.

This is true, on a personal level, in a group, on a nation, and even in the church, if we do not agree to walk together, according to God's plans and purposes, for better or for worse, in sickness and in health, for richer or for poorer, till death do us part.

Example prayer:

Lord, I take responsibility and repent for my sins, the sins of my forefathers, the sins of my people, and the sins of our nation, for rejecting God's chosen people, the Jews.

Lord, I also repent on behalf of the church, for the areas where the church has broken covenant, and has rejected God's chosen people, the Jews, and through these broken covenants has brought the consequences upon the people of the church.

Lord, I ask that you would awaken the church, bring conviction, restore righteousness and purity, and activate a passion for advancing the Kingdom of God here on earth[34] as in Heaven.

Lord, I repent on behalf of the government, for the broken covenants with the Native Americans and of the atrocities of wars that caused the spilling of blood and the loss of life.

---

[34] Matthew 6:10 Thy kingdom come. Thy will be done in earth, as it is in heaven.

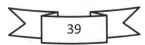

Understanding Emotional Healing

I ask, Lord, that you would break and destroy the curse of these sins and iniquities, and restore us to a covenant keeping people.

In Jesus Name, Amen.

Sexual Immorality (Caused by Compromise)

Sexual immorality is caused by violating the principles and the plans that God has for true intimacy.

Sexual immorality happens when people focus on their own fleshly desires and lusts[35] in the natural realm, instead of having true intimacy with God in the spiritual realm. They do not honor and glorify[36] God as being the Sovereign Lord of the Truth.

Sexual immorality is a result of compromise[37]. When people compromise God's truth, it opens themselves, their descendants, and their people group, to a false intimacy which allows sexual immorality to become a stronghold.

By compromising God's truth, they are actually rejecting the knowledge[38] of God.

---

[35] Romans 1:24 Wherefore God also gave them up to uncleanness through the lusts of their own hearts, to dishonour their own bodies between themselves:

[36] Romans 1:21-22 Because that, when they knew God, they glorified him not as God, neither were thankful; but became vain in their imaginations, and their foolish heart was darkened. Professing themselves to be wise, they became fools,

[37] Revelations 2:14 But I have a few things against thee, because thou hast therefore them that hold the doctrine of Balaam, who taught Balac to cast a stumbling block before the children of Israel, to eat things sacrificed unto idols, and to commit fornication.

[38] Hosea 4:6 My people are destroyed for lack of knowledge: because thou hast rejected knowledge, I will also

Identifying Ancient Strongholds

Sexual immorality includes but is not limited to:
- Sex outside of marriage
- Adultery
- Sexual immorality within marriage
- Masturbation
- Pornography
- Immodesty
- Homosexuality
- Incest
- Beastiality

Sexual immorality is a counterfeit supplied by the enemy to try to derail God's plan for deep relationship. To have a deep relationship with God and others, it is necessary to open up the heart.

Many people are unwilling to face the wounds of the heart, and therefore they try to live in denial, and begin to love the wages of unrighteousness[39].

The wages of unrighteousness is short-term pleasure for long term pain. The wages of righteousness is short-term pain for long-term pleasure.

Sexual immorality is used by the enemy to bring confusion and compromise in the lives of little children through abuse. This will cause them to have a difficulty to trust in God.

---

reject thee, that thou shalt be no priest to me: seeing thou hast forgotten the law of thy God, I will also forget thy children.

[39] 2 Peter 2:15 Which have forsaken the right way, and are gone astray, following the way of Balaam the son of Bosor, who loved the wages of unrighteousness;

Understanding Emotional Healing

Sexual abuse directed at small children will cause them to lose their voice, will cause them to feel alone, neglected, abandoned, and will cause wounds in their soul.

When they grow up, these soul wounds will mess up their marriage, if they are not taken care of.

With wounds in their souls, people will go around looking for love in all the wrong places, driven by a spirit of lust.

Sexual immorality is a performance-based plan of the enemy to keep people from being free.

This is the one of the deepest ways that the enemy is messing up people, because it is a perversion of the true intimacy that God designed us for.

The enemy is using this to advance the kingdom of darkness by creating more hurts, which makes people react.

Jesus wants to advance the Kingdom of God by creating a safe place that is protected and secure in the love and intimacy of God.

Example prayer:

Lord, I take responsibility and repent for my sins, the sins of my forefathers, the sins of my people, and the sins of our nation, for all forms of sexual immorality.

Identifying Ancient Strongholds

Lord, I repent for _____ (name the sin) _____ and I repent for the compromise that opened the door for this sexual immorality to gain access in my life.

Lord, I also repent on behalf of the church, for the areas where the church has compromised instead of standing for Truth.

Lord, I ask that You would awaken the church, bring conviction, restore righteousness and purity, and activate a passion for advancing the Kingdom of God here on earth[40] as in Heaven.

Lord, I repent on behalf of the government, for allowing compromise to open the door to homosexuality and other sexual immorality.

I ask, Lord, that You would break and destroy the curse of these sins and iniquities, and restore us to righteousness.

In Jesus Name, Amen.

Compromise

Throughout history the enemy has done everything he can to destroy God's plan for mankind. In the Garden of Eden the serpent came to Eve and tricked her into a compromise.

Balaam taught Balak how to mingle their women with the

---

[40] Matthew 6:10 Thy kingdom come. Thy will be done in earth, as it is in heaven.

Understanding Emotional Healing

Israelites, so they would compromise the blessings of God by allowing sexual immorality[41] to separate them from God.

In the wilderness, the devil offered Jesus a compromise. The devil took Jesus to an exceeding high mountain and showed him all the kingdoms of this world, and the glory[42] of them.

The devil told Jesus that all He has to do is fall down and worship the devil[43], and he would give Jesus everything.

If Jesus would have taken this offer He would have bypassed the cross, avoided the pain and suffering, and would have received the natural glory of the kingdoms of this world.

However by doing this, Jesus would have been disobedient to God, and it would have derailed mankind's opportunity to reconcile[44] with God.

Jesus told satan that it is written[45] thou shall worship the Lord thy God and Him only shalt thou serve.

(Today many people are taking satan's offer to bypass the cross, to avoid the pain and suffering, and to receive the natural

---

[41] Revelations 2:14 But I have a few things against thee, because thou hast therefore them that hold the doctrine of Balaam, who taught Balac to cast a stumbling block before the children of Israel, to eat things sacrificed unto idols, and to commit fornication.

[42] Matthew 4:8 Again, the devil taketh him up into an exceeding high mountain, and sheweth him all the kingdoms of the world, and the glory of them;

[43] Matthew 4:9 And saith unto him, All these things will I give thee, if thou wilt fall down and worship me.

[44] Romans 5:10 For if, when we were enemies, we were reconciled to God by the death of his Son, much more, being reconciled, we shall be saved by his life.

[45] Matthew 4:10 Then saith Jesus unto him, Get thee hence, Satan: for it is written, Thou shalt worship the Lord thy God, and him only shalt thou serve.

Identifying Ancient Strongholds

glory of the kingdoms of this world. This is keeping them from fulfilling God's plan in their life.)

Jesus went to the cross and did not compromise with the enemy in any way. This allows anyone, who accepts the sacrifice that Jesus paid for them, to be restored back to the original intent of God's purpose and plan for mankind.

After Jesus ascended into Heaven and the disciples were filled with the Holy Spirit, the believers were multiplied in vast numbers.

In spite of being persecuted, or maybe even because they were being persecuted, the truth was being spread all over the region. Christianity was flourishing because the believers refused to compromise even though it might cost them their lives[46].

https://en.wikipedia.org/wiki/Dirk_Willems

---

[46] Revelation 12:11 And they overcame him by the blood of the Lamb, and by the word of their testimony; and they loved not their lives unto the death.

Understanding Emotional Healing

In 1525, a group of people later called the Anabaptists devoted their lives to full surrender to God and His Kingdom.

Their goal was to live their lives, and be the church, as God had originally planned. With this decision the Christians were again being persecuted for their faith.

By the 1650's, the Anabaptists became weary of persecution and tired of suffering. Something had changed, and they no longer carried that unquenchable passion (because of rejecting the Holy Spirit).

They became inward focused to protect themselves, because they no longer had the fire to endure the persecution or to reach out to others.

Because France had been in a 30 year war their farmland had been devastated. They knew that the Anabaptists were hard-working people and they wanted them to come to restore the land.

They invited the Anabaptists to come to the Alsace Region of France, and offered them a peaceful solution to their persecuted life. By accepting this offer it appears like they compromised their mission to follow Jesus with all their heart.

Some of the benefits of receiving the offer were:
- No persecution
- Financial security
- Social acceptance

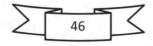

Identifying Ancient Strongholds

Some of the consequences of the compromise were:
- They were not allowed to have public meetings
- They were only allowed to gather in small groups
- They were not allowed to share their faith outside their own group

The Anabaptists agreed to this offer. After this they settled down and set their hearts to farming the land. They became known as the 'silent in the land'.

Because they agreed to compromise:
- They lost their power
- They became inward focused
- They gave up their inheritance

In Revelation chapter 3, Jesus is speaking to the church. He said that the church is lukewarm. He wants the church to be either cold or hot. Because the church is neither cold or hot, He will vomit it out of His mouth[47].

The church believed they had no problems, they were rich, they had many possessions, and they thought they didn't need anything.

However, Jesus is saying they did not know they were wretched, miserable, poor, blind, and naked[48].

---

[47] Revelation 3:15-16 I know thy works, that thou art neither cold nor hot: I would thou wert cold or hot. So then because thou art lukewarm, and neither cold nor hot, I will spue thee out of my mouth.

[48] Revelation 3:17 Because thou sayest, I am rich, and increased with goods, and have need of nothing; and knowest not that thou art wretched, and miserable, and poor, and blind, and naked:

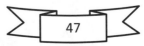

Understanding Emotional Healing

Jesus recommended that they buy gold that is tried in the fire[49] (faith that is tested by trials), so they could be rich (have Spiritual authority).

White raiment that they could be clothed with (purity), and that the shame of their nakedness would not appear (modesty), and their eyes would be anointed (Spiritual discernment) with eye salve so they could see (vision for the future).

Example prayer:

Lord, I take responsibility and repent for my sins, the sins of my forefathers, the sins of my people, and the sins of our nation, for all forms of compromise that opened the door for the enemy to infiltrate and dis-empower the church.

Lord, I repent on behalf of the church, for the areas where the church has compromised instead of standing for Truth. Lord, I also repent for lukewarmness in myself and in the church.

I ask, Lord, that You would break and destroy the curse of these sins and iniquities, and restore us to righteousness and truth.

Lord, we want to buy of You gold tried in the fire, that we may be rich, and we want to be clothed in the white raiment to cover the shame of our nakedness. Anoint our eyes with eye salve that we may see.

---

[49] Revelation 3:18 I counsel thee to buy of me gold tried in the fire, that thou mayest be rich; and white raiment, that thou mayest be clothed, and that the shame of thy nakedness do not appear; and annoint thine eyes with eye salve, that thou mayest see.

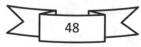

Identifying Ancient Strongholds

Lord, I ask that You would awaken the church, bring conviction, restore righteousness and purity, and activate a passion for advancing the Kingdom of God here on earth[50] as in Heaven.

In Jesus Name, Amen.

---

[50] Matthew 6:10 Thy kingdom come. Thy will be done in earth, as it is in heaven.

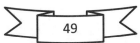

Understanding Emotional Healing

Matthew 6:10 Thy kingdom come. Thy will be done in earth, as it is in heaven.

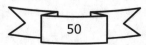

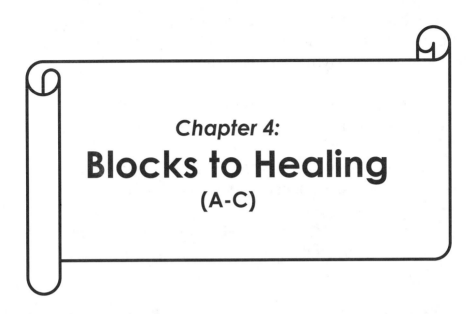

Chapter 4:
Blocks to Healing
(A-C)

When we think about blocks to healing, we are looking for things that are blocking the Divine flow of God's power. When these blockages are removed it allows the power of God's glory to flow through a person.

When the power of God is flowing through us it empowers us to live life in harmony with God. Only by experiencing this harmony with God can we experience the freedom that God intended for us to experience.

If there are many logs floating down a river, and they get jammed, usually it takes one or two logs, at a specific place, to be unjammed, and the whole pile of logs will start flowing again.

When a computer program gets a virus, it takes only one error for everything to be messed up.

Understanding Emotional Healing

Our heart and our brain works the same way. We are given the mind of Christ, but if we believe the lies of the enemy we will come up with the wrong answers (errors).

Just like the computer virus these lies are a virus of the enemy, designed to destroy our peace and our faith in God.

When we receive the free gift that Jesus paid for, when he died on the cross, we become adopted into God's family.

If we do not believe this we will not function as a person who has already conquered and won the victory. Instead we will function as a person who is defeated.

As we recognize the blockages and the lies that are separating us from God, we have the opportunity to repent for the lies and remove these blockages from our lives.

When we work with people we are listening, caring, and looking for the specific areas where their speech, their thought patterns, and their beliefs of the heart are not lining up with the mind of Christ and with the Truth.

The first step to helping somebody is to care about them from our heart. When they see that we care they will automatically begin to trust and feel safe to open up their heart.

Trust is a very important part of emotional healing, because it allows an opportunity for truth to combat the lies that the person is believing.

Blocks to Healing (A-C)

It allows an opportunity for others to point out their blockages and the areas that are not reconciling with the Truth. This will help them to get rid of all the lies they are believing, come into alignment with the Truth, and be completely free.

In the following chapters we are addressing some common blocks to healing, followed by prayers of repentance, and freedom from that specific block.

Abandonment

Abandonment is withdrawing one's support or help from a person, especially in spite of duty or responsibility. It is giving up, leaving, or ceasing to operate.

Abandonment is the willful forsaking or forgoing of parental duties. It is some form of clear action that is taken, to indicate that the owner no longer wants his or her property.

Abandonment is to leave, forsake, desert, yield control of, withdraw from, or cast away. It is to withdraw protection, support, or help from our family.

Abandonment is leaving of a person to whom one is bound by special relation such as a wife, husband, or child.

Abandonment issues arise when children are raised with chronic loss, without the psychological or physical protection they need and certainly deserve.

It is common for children that are abandoned to internalize incredible fear.

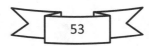

Understanding Emotional Healing

Not receiving the necessary psychological or physical protection equals abandonment. And living with repeated abandonment experiences creates toxic shame.

Shame arises from the painful message implied in the abandonment, such as:
- "You are not important."
- "You have no value."

Physical abandonment occurs when the physical conditions necessary for thriving are then replaced by:
- Lack of appropriate supervision.
- Inadequate provision of nutrition and meals.
- Inadequate clothing, housing, heat, or shelter.
- Physical and/or sexual abuse.

Emotional abandonment occurs when parents do not provide the emotional conditions and the emotional environment necessary for healthy development.

This causes a child to start believing that they need to hide a part of who they are in order to be accepted, or to not be rejected.

Having to hide a part of yourself means:
- Believing it is not okay to make a mistake.
- Believing it is not okay to show feelings.
- Being told the way you feel is not true.
- Being told you have nothing to cry about.
- Being told if you don't stop crying, I will really give you something to cry about.

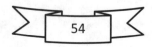

Blocks to Healing (A-C)

- Being told that really didn't hurt.
- Being told you have nothing to be angry about.
- Believing it is not okay to have needs.
- Believing everyone else's needs are more important than yours.
- Believing it is not okay to be successful.
- Accomplishments are not acknowledged, or are many times discounted.

Other acts of abandonment occur when:
- Children cannot live up to the expectations of their parents. These expectations are often unrealistic, and not age appropriate.
- Children are held responsible for other people's behavior. They may be consistently blamed for the actions and feelings of their parents.
- Disapproval toward children is aimed at their entire beings, or identity, rather than a particular behavior. For example, telling a child he is worthless when he does not do his homework, or she is never going to be a good athlete because she missed the final catch of the game.

Abandonment issues can only be overcome when a person realizes that God never abandoned[51] them.

God did not approve of the abandonment that we went through and He is patiently waiting until we are willing to turn the abandonment issues over to Him.

---

[51] Hebrews 13:5 Let your conversation be without covetousness; and be content with such things as ye have: for he hath said, I will never leave thee nor forsake thee.

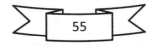

Understanding Emotional Healing

Abandonment is overcome when we accept our adoption[52] into God's family. We get adopted into God's family by repenting of our sins and receiving what Jesus paid for at the cross.

Jesus died so that we can be reconciled[53] with God, and we can be accepted into His family, and fulfill the purposes that God has for our lives.

Example prayer:

Lord, I forgive everyone who has ever hurt me, misused me, mistreated me, abused me, abandoned me, rejected me, or who wasn't there for me when I needed them. It doesn't mean what they did was right, it just means that I choose to give it to You, Lord, and I forgive them.

*Lord, Your Word says to bless those that curse me, so I choose to bless **ALL** the people who have transgressed against me.*

And Lord, I forgive myself for every mistake that I have ever made, and I choose to receive the acceptance that You have for me.

Lord, Your Word says that I can be adopted into Your family. I repent of all my sins, and bring them to the cross.

---

[52] Romans 8:15 For ye have not received the spirit of bondage again to fear; but ye have received the Spirit of adoption, whereby we cry, Abba, Father.

[53] 2 Corinthians 5:18 And all things are of God, who hath reconciled us to himself by Jesus Christ, and hath given us the ministry of reconciliation;

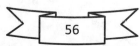

Blocks to Healing (A-C)

Thank you, Jesus, for dying on the cross for my sins, and making a way for me to be reconciled with God.

Lord, I ask that You would hold me in Your arms, protect me, love me, and heal me from the abandonment issues in my heart.

In Jesus Name, Amen.

Accusations

Accusations are charges or claims that someone has done something illegal or wrong. It is an allegation that a person is guilty of some fault, offense, or crime. An accusation is a justification not to forgive.

It is important to remember that an accusation comes about when someone thinks another person has done something wrong or committed a crime. However, it doesn't necessarily mean that the person is guilty.

Instead of accusations, it is better to help a person to resolve their problems, by bringing them to God for healing. It is not our duty to accuse people, but rather to pray for them and intercede for them. After we have prayed about this, we can speak to them in love. Many times the picture changes when we find out the facts.

If accusations are coming against you, first take them to God and ask Him to show you if there is any truth in it. If so, repent and realign with God's plan. If the accusations are not true,

Understanding Emotional Healing

forgive the people for bringing the accusations, and turn them over to God.

Most accusations can be resolved in the spirit realm, without ever speaking about them in the natural realm. Only confront the accusations in the natural after you have prayed and feel peace in your heart to do so.

Example prayer:

Lord, I take authority over and cancel all accusations, condemnations, insinuations, and judgments that are coming against me.

Lord, I bring them all to You and ask that You would apply the blood of Jesus to destroy all these curses.

Lord, Your Word says to bless those that curse[54] me, so I ask that You would send blessings to where ever these curses are coming from.

In Jesus Name, Amen.

Addictions

Addictions are when people continue to repeat certain behaviors despite harmful consequences.

---

[54] Matthew 5:44 But I say unto you, Love your enemies, bless them that curse you, do good to them that hate you, and pray for them which despitefully use you, and persecute you;

Blocks to Healing (A-C)

When most people think about addictions they think about substance abuse such as alcohol, tobacco, or other drugs.

However, in recent years scientists have spent more time studying what's known as behavioral addiction. This includes lack of control over one's actions, obsessive compulsive behavior, and continuing to do something despite negative consequences.

Addictions can include, but are not limited to:
- Alcohol
- Drugs and medications
- Gambling
- Negativity
- Self injury
- Sex (physical or mental)
- Tobacco

For some addictions, the action itself is considered socially acceptable making the addiction harder to identify and deal with.

In fact, some behaviors are so common that an addiction can easily go by unnoticed. Examples of this can be:
- Exercise
- Food
- Internet
- Money
- Religion
- Shopping
- Social Media
- Sports
- Television
- Work

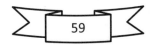

Understanding Emotional Healing

What causes addictions? People look to addictions to try to cover the pain and fill the hole in their heart. It is looking for love in all the wrong places.

Addictions are an attempt to feel good by external means, instead of looking internally to see what is really going on in the heart. It is a cover-up. Addictions are associated with denial.

Addictions are often connected to rebellion, especially towards God. This causes a person to seek false intimacy in things instead of **true intimacy** with God.

To overcome addictions, it is necessary to think back to when the addictions started, to see what was going on in our heart at the time the addiction started.

Many times we will find a decision or a vow, connected to the beginning of the addiction, that allows it to keep a hold on us.

Only by dealing with the roots[55] of the addictions can a person have long-term success of overcoming them. Otherwise it is a continued management effort and often a losing battle.

Example prayer:

Lord, I take responsibility and repent for the rebellion in my heart that allowed the addictions to take root.

Lord, I repent for the decisions and the vows that I made against Your plans for my life.

---

[55] Matthew 3:10 And now also the axe is laid unto the root of the trees: therefore every tree which bringeth not forth good fruit is hewn down, and cast into the fire.

Blocks to Healing (A-C)

Lord, I repent for attempting to feel good, using other means, instead of facing the issues[56] of my heart.

Lord, please reveal to me what was going on in my heart when the addictions started. **(Pause and allow God to speak to your heart at this time before continuing).**

Lord, I ask that You cleanse me from_____(name the roots)_____ and _____(name the addictions)_____ and all unrighteousness. Please remove them from me and help me to live my life completely for You.

Lord, I receive the gift of salvation that you have supplied for me by dying on the cross. Please help me to receive this freedom into my heart, and then allow it to work out[57] into the natural.

In Jesus Name, Amen.

Anger

Anger is related to a person's psychological interpretation of having been offended, wronged, or denied. Anger is part of the fight or flight brain response to a perceived threat of harm. Anger can negatively affect personal or social well-being.

Anger is always a secondary emotion. Anger focuses on

---

[56] Proverbs 4:23 Keep thy heart with all diligence; for out of it are the issues of life.

[57] Philippians 2:12 Wherefore, my beloved, as ye have always obeyed, not as in my presence only, but now much more in my absence, work out your own salvation with fear and trembling.

Understanding Emotional Healing

blaming other people or circumstances for our problems, instead of taking responsibility for our own well-being.

Anger is an intimidation tactic to get people to back away from the pain that is surfacing. Most people think anger helps them, because it makes other people back off when a lot of emotion and dramatic force is displayed.

The reason people need anger is to block their true feelings from coming to the surface. When we are willing to face the truth we can get rid of the anger, and take an honest look at what is really going on deep down inside of our heart.

When we get honest and open[58] with ourselves, with each other, and get honest with God, then true healing can begin to happen.

When anger is no longer an option we can begin to start dealing with the fears and insecurities that were covered over by the anger.

Example prayer:

Lord, I take responsibility and repent for allowing anger to operate in my life, and I bring it all to You at the cross.

Lord, I ask that You would apply the blood of Jesus to the anger and remove it from my life.

---

[58] James 5:16 Confess your faults one to another, and pray one for another, that ye may be healed. The effectual fervent prayer of a righteous man availeth much.

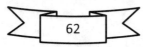

Blocks to Healing (A-C)

Lord, I am willing to face the truth of what is going on in my heart.

In Jesus Name, Amen.

Anxiety

Anxiety is an unpleasant state of inner turmoil, often accompanied by nervous behavior, such as pacing back and forth. It is a feeling of fear, unease, and worry.

Anxiety is a form of fear. However, instead of the fear being real it is an overreaction to an unreal or imagined danger. It is a fear gone wild.

Anxiety is a sense of dread about something 'out there' that seems threatening, but in reality it may not even be there.

Anxiety is usually unrealistic or out of proportion with what may be expected in a situation.

Anxiety sufferers expect failure and disaster to the point that it interferes with daily functions like work, school, sleep, social activities, and relationships.

To overcome anxiety, the Bible tells us to take no thought for tomorrow[59] and to be anxious for nothing[60]. To do this, we will

---

[59] Matthew 6:34 Take therefore no thought for the morrow: for the morrow shall take thought for the things of itself. Sufficient unto the day is the evil thereof.

[60] Philippians 4:6 Be anxious for nothing, but in everything by prayer and supplication, with thanksgiving, let your requests be made known to God; NKJV

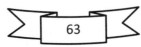

Understanding Emotional Healing

need to trust[61] in the Lord with all our heart, and not lean on our own brain (understanding).

Example prayer:

Lord, I take responsibility and repent for not trusting You with all my heart.

Lord, I repent for allowing anxiety to operate in my life. I don't need this anxiety anymore. Please remove it from me and help me to remember to trust in You.

Lord, I choose to trust in You with all my heart, instead of leaning on my brain. Please fill me with Your peace.

Lord, Your Word says that Your strength is made perfect in weakness[62]. I give You my weakness in exchange for Your perfection.

In Jesus Name, Amen.

Bitterness

Bitterness is often caused by severe grief, anguish, or disappointment, mixed with resentment.

It comes from blaming God for something that does not go our own way and it will damage our relationship with God.

---

[61] Proverbs 3:5 Trust in the Lord with all thine heart; and lean not unto thine own understanding.
[62] 2 Corinthians 12:9 And he said unto me, My grace is sufficient for thee: for my strength is made perfect in weakness. Most gladly therefore will I rather glory in my infirmities, that the power of Christ may rest upon me.

Blocks to Healing (A-C)

Bitterness directs our focus onto our problem, instead of keeping our focus on God.

Bitterness and discouragement are two of the enemy's favorite ways to draw us away from God. Bitterness takes root in the heart and spreads its poison to choke out every Godly trait there.

In the Bible, in the book of James, it warns us to beware of any root[63] of bitterness taking hold and defiling many. Bitterness tends to cause us to look for other people to agree with our offenses.

Our bitterness tends to punish our family and friends, because they will feel a need to tiptoe around our touchiness. This can cause them to feel like they need to walk around on eggshells when they are around us.

This, in turn, can cause them to tend to want to leave us alone which can cause us much loneliness.

The way to overcome bitterness is by going to God and asking Him to be in charge of our justice. We've been hurt and we want justice but that is His job, not ours.

He is the One who makes things right. When we return that responsibility to God, we will feel a heavy load[64] come off our back.

---

[63] Hebrews 12:15 Looking diligently lest and a man fail of the grace of God; lest any root of bitterness springing up trouble you, and thereby many be defiled;

[64] Matthew 11:30 For my yoke is easy, and my burden is light.

Understanding Emotional Healing

When we remember that bitterness is a choice, then we will learn to choose peace and contentment[65] instead.

Example prayer:

Lord, I take responsibility and repent for all the bitterness and offenses that I have carried in my heart.

Lord, I ask that You would remove the root of bitterness from my life, and that You would heal the people who have been defiled by my bitterness.

Lord, I choose to forgive and bless the people in every situation who have offended me.

Lord, I ask that You would cleanse my heart from all unrighteousness and purify my life.

Lord, I now choose peace and contentment for my life.

In Jesus Name, Amen.

Blame

Blame is a self-defense that we use to avoid the responsibility for our own healing and for our own actions.

This causes us to focus on other people or circumstances to justify our own shortcomings.

---

[65] 1 Timothy 6:6 But godliness with contentment is great gain.

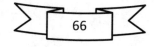

Blocks to Healing (A-C)

Many people have difficulty taking responsibility for their own bitterness.

If we have a need to blame others we are putting the focus on them, and therefore it keeps us from being able to be healed.

In every situation that we face, no matter what it is, we have the opportunity to be free. If it was something that we did wrong, we can repent.

If it was something that somebody else did wrong, we can forgive. This brings us back into Divine alignment.

Example prayer:

Lord, I take responsibility and repent for blaming other people for the problems in my life.

I recognize that if I trust You, Lord, all things[66] will work together for good.

Lord, I am willing to face the truth of what is going on in my heart.

In Jesus Name, Amen.

---

[66] Romans 8:28 and we know that all things work together for good to them that love God, to them who are the called according to his purpose.

Understanding Emotional Healing

Burnout

Burnout is a state of emotional, mental, and physical exhaustion caused by excessive and prolonged stress. It occurs when we feel overwhelmed and unable to meet constant demands.

As the stress continues, we begin to lose the interest or motivation that led us to take on a certain role in the first place.

Burnout reduces our productivity and saps our energy, leaving us feeling increasingly helpless, hopeless, and resentful. Eventually, we may feel that we have nothing more to give.

Burnout is a feeling of not being enough. People experiencing burnout often don't see any hope of positive change in their situations.

Burnout is caused by adrenal fatigue or exhaustion. It is exhaustion as a result of longtime stress.

Example prayer:

Lord, I take responsibility and repent for allowing stress and exhaustion to bring burnout into my life.

Lord, I choose to trust You with all my problems, all my deadlines, all my projects, my entire family, and my entire future.

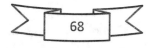

Blocks to Healing (A-C)

Lord, I choose to surrender completely to You in every area of my life and I choose to enter into Your rest[67].

In Jesus Name, Amen.

Comparisons

Comparisons is looking to see if we're above or below someone else.

To overcome comparisons we need to look to Jesus to see what He wants us to do, instead of comparing ourselves to others.

True humility is doing exactly what God asks us to do instead of comparing ourselves to others.

The only way we can be truly united in the body of Christ, as one church, is if we all go to Jesus.

If we get our instructions from Jesus, we can do what he says and grow together.

We are not equal in our gifts or equal in our abilities, but we are equal in who we are in Christ.

---

[67] Hebrews 4:9-11 There remaineth therefore a rest to the people of God. For he that is entered into his rest, he also had ceased from his own works, as God did from his. That us labour therefore to enter into that rest, lest any man fall after the same example of unbelief.

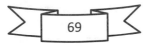

Understanding Emotional Healing

Example prayer:

Lord, I take responsibility and repent for allowing envy and jealousy to operate in my life.

Lord, I repent for comparing myself to others, what others have, and what they can do.

Lord, please remove all comparisons from my life and help me to keep my focus on You.

Lord, I ask for the blood of Jesus to cleanse me from all unrighteousness.

Lord, I choose to submit[68] to You, and resist the devil, so that he will flee.

In Jesus Name, Amen.

Condemnations

Condemnation is the act of declaring something awful or evil. It is laying a heavy moral blame on someone.

Condemnation is an expression of strong disapproval. It is to pronounce unfavorable or severe judgment against.

When condemnation comes upon somebody, it will always take them to one ditch or the other.

---

[68] James 4:7 Submit yourselves therefore to God. Resist the devil, and he will flee from you.

Blocks to Healing (A-C)

It is not our duty to condemn anybody, but rather to help them reconcile with God.

If condemnations are coming against us we can take them to God and ask Him to show us if there is any truth in it. If so, we can repent and realign with God's plan.

If the condemnations are not true we can forgive the people for bringing the condemnations, and turn them over to God.

Example prayer:

Lord, I take authority over and cancel all accusations, condemnations[69], insinuations, and judgments coming against me.

Lord, I bring them to You and ask that You would apply the blood of Jesus to destroy all these curses.

Lord, Your Word says to bless those that curse[70] me, so I ask that You would send blessings to where ever these curses are coming from.

In Jesus Name, Amen.

---

[69] Romans 8:1 There is therefore now no condemnation to them which are in Christ Jesus, who walk not after the flesh, but after the Spirit.

[70] Matthew 5:44 But I say unto you, Love your enemies, bless them that curse you, do good to them that hate you, and pray for them which despitefully use you, and persecute you;

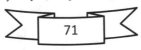

Understanding Emotional Healing

Control

Control is to exercise authoritative or dominating influence over. It is the authority or ability to manage or direct.

Control in itself is not wrong. However, when we begin to use it against God, or God's will, or to manipulate people, it severely damages our lives as well as the lives of other people.

This can be defined by a term called 'control freak' which is ruled by a spirit of control.

A 'control freak' is a person who attempts to dictate how everything around them is done.

'Control freaks' are often perfectionists, defending themselves against their own inner vulnerabilities. They do this in the belief that if they are not in total control, they risk exposing themselves once more to childhood insecurities.

This is a method of self protection, often used to cover pain.

Such a person will manipulate and pressure others to change to avoid having to change themselves. They will use power over others to escape their inner emptiness.

A person with a control spirit has an unhealthy need to influence others. This can be manifested through leaders who are insecure in their leadership. It will also manifest through people who are trying to control their situations to not get hurt again.

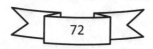

Blocks to Healing (A-C)

To overcome the spirit of control, we can submit ourselves one to another[71] and focus on what God wants to do with our life, and then surrender[72] to God's plan and release others to God.

Example prayer:

Lord, I take responsibility and repent for allowing a spirit of control to operate in my life.

Lord, I choose to surrender my life to You, and I allow You to completely take over. I release everyone to You and trust You to take care of every situation.

Use me in whatever way You want to, Lord.

In Jesus Name, Amen.

Covetousness

Covetousness is the strong desire to have that which belongs to another. It is an excessive desire for riches, money, power, or ability, especially that which belongs to someone else. It is an extreme eagerness to possess something.

Covetousness is a feeling of overwhelming desire to have something that is possessed by another. It is a longing to appropriate what rightfully belongs to someone else. It is a strong desire after the possession of worldly things.

---

[71] if these events 5:21 Submitting yourselves one to another in the fear of God.

[72] James 4:7 Submit yourselves therefore to God. Resist the devil, and he will flee from you.

Understanding Emotional Healing

To overcome covetousness, it is important to seek after Godly contentment[73] instead of pursuing natural possessions or abilities.

Example prayer:

Lord, I take responsibility and repent for allowing covetousness to operate in my life.

Lord, I repent for desiring possessions or abilities to fill the void in my life. Please remove all covetousness from my life.

Lord, I ask for the blood of Jesus to cleanse me from all unrighteousness and give me peace and contentment.

*Lord, I ask You to **take over**[74] my life.*

Lord, I choose to submit[75] to You, and resist the devil, so that he will flee.

In Jesus Name, Amen.

---

[73] 1 Timothy 6:6 But godliness with contentment is great gain.

[74] Philippians 2:13 for it is God which worketh in you both to will and to do his good pleasure.

[75] James 4:7 Submit yourselves therefore to God. Resist the devil, and he will flee from you.

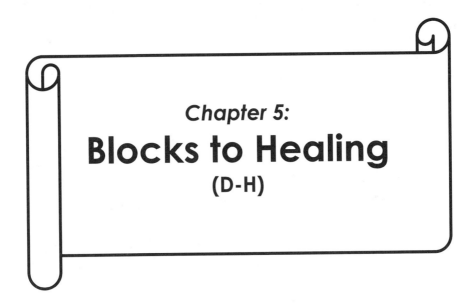

Chapter 5:
Blocks to Healing
(D-H)

Death Wishes

Death wishes and agreements with death, including suicidal thoughts, are a rebellion to God's plan for our life. God tells us in His Word to **choose life**[76].

When we make a death wish a part of our body starts to shut down and die, while another part of our body is trying to live.

In the natural we call this cancer. When people have cancer their own cells are fighting against themselves.

---

[76] Deuteronomy 30:19 I call Heaven and earth to record this day against you, that I have set before you life and death, blessing and cursing: therefore choose life, that both thou and thy seed may live:

Understanding Emotional Healing

Death wishes come when hope is deferred[77]. (See hopelessness).

<u>Example prayer:</u>

Lord, I repent for all death wishes, agreements with death, and all suicidal thoughts.

Lord, I take responsibility and repent for not believing that You are big enough to handle my problems.

Lord, please remove all hopelessness and discouragement from my life, and help me to see the situation at hand from Your point of view.

Lord, I choose to believe in, and connect to, the hope that You have for me.

*Lord, I choose **LIFE**. I choose to surrender to Your plans for my life, and to focus on living my life to the fullest potential that You have for me.*

In Jesus Name, Amen.

Denial

Denial consists of the refusal to accept a past or present reality. It is one of the most common defense mechanisms used to hide from the truth.

---

[77] Proverbs 13:12 Hope deferred maketh the heart sick: but when the desire cometh, it is a tree of life.

Blocks to Healing (D-H)

Denial is an outright refusal to admit or recognize that something has occurred, or is currently occurring.

Denial functions to protect the ego from things that the individual cannot cope with. It requires a substantial amount of energy to keep these unacceptable feelings from coming to the surface.

Many people live in such a state of denial that it is hard for them to face what is truly going on in their life and in their heart. Only by getting rid of denial and being willing to face the truth can true healing begin.

Many people will ignore the reality of their problems, while other people may plainly see and need to bear the consequences of the denied problem.

A person that is living in denial is often unaware of the true situation. To overcome this, it is important that we are willing to be open and teachable[78], and allow other people to speak into our life.

Example prayer:

Lord, I take responsibility and repent for living in denial.

Lord, I give You permission to expose all the lies that I am believing, and bring them to the surface for healing.

---

[78] John 14:26 But the Comforter, which is the Holy Ghost, whom the Father will send in my name, he shall teach you all things, and bring all things to your remembrance, whatsoever I have said unto you.

Understanding Emotional Healing

Lord, I am willing to face the truth[79] of what is going on in my heart.

Lord, I ask that You would remove all denial from my life, and help me to face reality and take responsibility for my life.

In Jesus Name, Amen.

Depression

Depression may be described as feeling sad, blue, unhappy, miserable, or down in the dumps. It is a state of sadness, downswings in mood, or normal reactions to life's struggles, setbacks, and disappointments. It can affect a person's thoughts, behaviors, feelings, and sense of well-being.

Depressed people may feel sad, anxious, empty, hopeless, worried, helpless, worthless, guilty, irritable, hurt, or restless.

They may lose interest in activities that were once pleasurable, experience loss of appetite or overeating, have problems concentrating, remembering details, or making decisions, and may contemplate or attempt suicide. It may be a reaction to certain life events.

Some people describe depression as "living in a black hole" or having a feeling of impending doom. It can be a downward spiral.

---

[79] John 8:32 And ye shall know the truth, and the truth shall make you free.

Blocks to Healing (D-H)

Depression will set in and establish a stronghold when hopelessness is allowed to continue in our life.

Depression is anger turned inward.

To overcome depression, first deal with the hopelessness.

Hopelessness is not seeing any possibility of a solution. It is believing things are impossible.

Hopelessness is the despair we feel when we have lost hope of ever achieving comfort or success. It is the feeling that everything is wrong and nothing will turn out right.

Hopelessness comes in when a happening or event breaks our spirit or ability to function. It is the moment we believe that everything in our world is wrong, and there is absolutely nothing we can do about it.

Hopelessness is a feeling that conditions will never improve, and there is no solution to our problem.

Some expressions that people make that come from hopelessness:
- "Things will never get better."
- "There are no solutions to my problems."
- "I will never be happy again."
- "I will never get over what happened."
- "I don't see things ever improving."
- "There is no point in trying anymore."
- "I just want to give up."

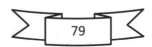

Understanding Emotional Healing

- "Things are hopeless."
- "I feel so helpless."
- "There is no hope for me."
- "What do I have to look forward to?"
- "The future is empty for me."
- "I see things getting worse in the future."
- "Everything is going downhill."
- "I will never get back to the way I was."
- "It's too late for me."
- "There is nothing that I can do to make things better."

If we are absolutely convinced that life is hopeless, then we won't do anything to help ourselves. But no matter how hopeless it seems, there are things we can do – right now – that can help us find a way out.

To overcome hopelessness, we need to work on changing our perception[80] and attitude toward the problem. Even though we can't change the circumstances in which we work or live, we can always change our perception and our attitude.

In order to change our perception, we need to start looking at the situation from God's point of view. Is it something that is too much for God? If so, we need a bigger God.

When we focus on our problem being bigger than God, we have no choice but to surrender to the problem.

However, when we focus on God being bigger than our

---

[80] Isaiah 55:9 For as the heavens are higher than the earth, so are my ways higher than your ways, and my thoughts than your thoughts.

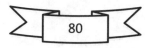

Blocks to Healing (D-H)

problems, then we will have the ability and the opportunity to surrender to God.

Example prayer:

Lord, I take responsibility and repent for not believing that You are big[81] enough to handle my problems.

Lord, please remove all hopelessness and discouragement from my life, and help me to see the situation at hand from Your point of view.

Lord, I repent for allowing depression to operate in my life. Please remove all depression from me and help me to keep my eyes fixed on You, Lord.

*Lord, I choose to believe in, and connect to, the **HOPE** that You have for me.*

In Jesus Name, Amen.

Discouragement

Discouragement is a feeling of having lost hope or confidence. It is a feeling of despair in the face of obstacles. It can come from believing that everything is wrong and nothing will turn out right.

---

[81] Romans 8:37–39 Nay, in all these things we are more than conquerors through him that loved us. For I am persuaded, that neither death, nor life, nor angels, nor principalities, nor powers, nor things present, nor things to come, nor height, nor depth, nor any other creature, shall be able to separate us from the love of God, which is in Christ Jesus our Lord.

Understanding Emotional Healing

Discouragement and bitterness are two of the enemy's favorite ways to draw us away from God. Discouragement is often caused by fear of failure, and is a form of rebellion to God's plan for our life.

Discouragement is a choice. If we feel discouraged it's because we have chosen to feel that way. No one is forcing us to feel bad.

We can make a choice to trust God and do what's right in spite of our feelings.

To overcome discouragement, we need to work on changing our perception and attitude toward the problem. Even though we can't change the circumstances in which we work or live, we can always change our perception and our attitude.

In order to change our perception, we need to start looking at the situation from God's point of view. Is it something that is too much for God? If so, we need a bigger[82] God.

When we focus on our problem being bigger than God we have no choice but to surrender to the problem.

However, when we focus on God being bigger than our problem, then we will have the ability and the opportunity to surrender to God.

---

[82] Romans 8:37–39 Nay, in all these things we are more than conquerors through him that loved us. For I am persuaded, that neither death, nor life, nor angels, nor principalities, nor powers, nor things present, nor things to come, nor height, nor depth, nor any other creature, shall be able to separate us from the love of God, which is in Christ Jesus our Lord.

Blocks to Healing (D-H)

Example prayer:

Lord, I take responsibility and repent for not believing that You are big enough to handle my problems.

Lord, please remove all discouragement from my life, and help me to see the situation at hand from Your point of view.

In Jesus Name, Amen.

Double-Mindedness

Double-mindedness is the act of having two conflicting programs running in our head at the same time.

One program may be wanting to do the right thing and connect to God, and the other program is believing lies and rebelling against God.

A double minded man is unstable in all his ways[83]. For instance it is like a cancer in our body, where part of us wants to live and part of us wants to die.

To overcome double-mindedness, it is necessary to make a decision on what is Truth, and then eliminate the lies that do not line up with Truth[84].

---

[83] James 1:8 A double minded man is unstable in all his ways.
[84] John 14:6 Jesus saith unto him, I am the way, the truth, and the life: no man cometh unto the Father, but by me.

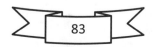

Understanding Emotional Healing

<u>Example prayer:</u>

Lord, I take responsibility and repent for double-mindedness[85] and for allowing the lies to live in my mind.

Lord, please remove all the double-mindedness from my life and help me to remember to walk in Truth.

I now choose to have my mind set on You, Lord, and I choose to function with my heart fixed on You.

In Jesus Name, Amen.

Envy

Envy is the resentment which occurs when someone lacks another's quality, achievement, or possession, and wishes that the other lacked it too.

Not only is the envious person rendered unhappy by this, but they also wish to inflict misfortune on others.

Envy is unreasonable, irrational, imprudent, and vicious. It is a feeling of discontentment or covetousness with regard to another's advantages, successes, possessions, etc.

Envy and jealousy are often used interchangeably in common usage, but the words stand for two distinct emotions.

---

[85] James 4:8 Draw nigh to God, and he will draw nigh to you. Cleanse your hands, ye sinners; and purify your hearts, ye double minded.

Blocks to Healing (D-H)

Jealousy is the fear of losing someone or something that we are attached to. Envy is the resentment caused by another person having something that we do not have, but desire for ourselves.

Envy is the result of comparing ourselves to things in the natural realm[86], and feeling like we come out with the short end of the stick.

Where envy[87] and strife are, there is confusion and every evil work. Envy causes rottenness of the bones[88].

To overcome envy it is important to realign with God and agree with His plans for our life.

Example prayer:

Lord, I take responsibility and repent for allowing envy and jealousy to operate in my life.

Lord, I repent for comparing myself with others and what others have. Please remove all envy and jealousy from my life.

Lord, I ask for the blood of Jesus to cleanse me from all unrighteousness and fill me with contentment.

---

[86] 2 Corinthians 10:12b ...but they measuring themselves by themselves, and comparing themselves among themselves, are not wise.

[87] James 3:16 For where envying and strife is, there is confusion and every evil work.

[88] Proverbs 14:30 A sound heart is the life of the flesh: but envy the rottenness of the bones.

Understanding Emotional Healing

Lord, I choose to submit[89] to You, and resist the devil, so that he will flee.

In Jesus Name, Amen.

'Fantasy World'

A 'fantasy world[90]' is something that is conceived in the imagination to escape into, instead of facing reality. It is creating our own world and living in denial in an attempt to avoid the truth.

Many people create a 'fantasy world' at an early age in their life to escape the trauma and abuse that they are exposed to.

Later on in life, it is difficult to receive the truth, because it clashes with our 'fantasy world'.

To find true freedom, it is important to destroy our 'fantasy world' and to face reality.

When we face and embrace the truth, even though it can be extremely painful, the truth will make us free[91].

---

[89] James 4:7 Submit yourselves therefore to God. Resist the devil, and he will flee from you.

[90] 2 Corinthians 10:5 Casting down imaginations, and every high thing that exalteth itself against the knowledge of God, and bringing into captivity every thought to the obedience of Christ;

[91] John 8:32 And ye shall know the truth, and the truth shall make you free.

Blocks to Healing (D-H)

<u>Example prayer:</u>

Lord, I take responsibility and repent for creating a 'fantasy world' to block out the Truth.

Lord, I give You permission to destroy my 'fantasy world' completely.

Lord, I ask that You would help me to face and embrace the reality in my life.

*Lord, please help me to sort through the pain in my heart, and bring it **all** to You.*

Lord, I choose to receive the Truth, and allow the Truth to make me free.

In Jesus Name, Amen.

Fear

Fear is a reaction to a real or threatened danger. It can be a manipulating and controlling factor in an individual's life.

Fear almost always relates to future events, such as worsening of a situation, or continuation of a situation that is unacceptable. It can also be an instant reaction to something presently happening.

Many people believe that fear is an emotion, however, fear is actually a spirit. The Bible tells us that God has not given us the

Understanding Emotional Healing

spirit of fear, but of power, and of love, and a sound mind[92]. Also, it says perfect love casts out fear[93].

We cannot cast out an emotion. We can only cast out a spirit. So fear is a spirit that messes with our emotions.

Fear is a form of faith in the wrong source and going in the wrong direction. Whatever we fear has permission to happen in our life.

Using fear is like hiring our enemy to guard our back door, and then wondering why we are not safe.

What is the physiology of fear, and how does it affect us in the natural?

The amygdala, located behind the pituitary gland, is the part of the limbic system that generates the secretion of hormones connected to fear and aggression.

As these hormones are released by the amygdala into the body it puts us into a state of alertness, in which we are ready to move, run, fight, etc.

This defensive response is known as the 'fight or flight mode' and is regulated by the hypothalamus gland. One of the functions of the hypothalamus gland is to determine if someone is in fear or at peace.

---

[92] 2 Timothy 1:7 For God hath not given us the spirit of fear; but of power, and of love, and of a sound mind.

[93] 1 John 4:18 There is no fear in love; but perfect love casteth out fear: because fear hath torment. He that feareth is not made perfect in love.

Blocks to Healing (D-H)

When it detects fear, it changes the hormonal balance, and the chemical balance in our body.

The adrenal glands will then release hormones, including adrenaline and cortisol. This gives us instant power and superhuman strength.

If there is an emergency, we can run faster than we ever ran before, jump higher than we ever jumped before, or lift more than we ever lifted before.

For example, when there is an accident, four men may be able to lift a car up off of somebody. Later, twelve men may not be able to lift that same car.

However, when cortisol is released at high levels for an extended period of time, it can be toxic to our system. For this reason, it is important to return to peace as soon as possible, after the emergency is over.

When we live in constant fear the hypothalamus gland will continue to release cortisol instead of returning us back to normal hormonal and chemical balance.

A doctor may tell us that we have a chemical imbalance or hormonal imbalance and put us on medication. This can temporarily balance our hormones or chemicals.

However, it does not resolve our fear issues. Unless the fear issues are resolved, we will continue to need our medications adjusted regularly.

Understanding Emotional Healing

When our fear issues are resolved and our body comes back into balance, our doctor will automatically adjust our medications, and eventually take us off the medications when it is safe to do so.

Some examples of fear are:
- Fear of flying
- Fear of heights
- Fear of clowns
- Fear of intimacy
- Fear of death
- Fear of rejection
- Fear of people
- Fear of snakes
- Fear of failure
- Fear of driving
- Fear of success
- Fear of demons
- Fear of cockroaches
- Fear of spiders
- Fear of water
- Fear of enclosed spaces
- Fear of tunnels
- Fear of bridges
- Fear of needles
- Fear of authority
- Fear of being deceived
- Fear of being alone
- Fear of cancer
- Fear of childbirth
- Fear of confinement

Blocks to Healing (D-H)

- Fear of confrontations
- Fear of crowds
- Fear of public speaking
- Fear of going crazy
- Fear of man[94]
- Fear of illness
- Fear of insanity
- Fear of drowning
- Fear of miscarriages
- Fear of making wrong decisions
- Fear of marriage
- Fear of nightmares
- Fear of pain
- Fear of rape
- Fear of responsibility
- Fear of satan
- Fear of sex
- Fear of storms
- Fear of suffering
- Fear of the future
- Fear of witchcraft
- Fear of...

In God's Kingdom we cannot stay fearful. God is love and perfect love casts out fear.

When fear first comes to us it comes in the form of a thought. The Bible talks about taking every thought captive[95], and bringing it to the obedience of Christ.

---

[94] Proverbs 29:25 The fear of man bringeth a snare: but whoso putteth his trust in the LORD shall be safe.

[95] 2 Corinthians 10:5 Casting down imaginations, and every high thing that exalteth itself against the knowledge of God, and bringing into captivity every thought to the obedience of Christ;

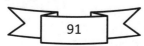

Understanding Emotional Healing

It can be helpful to see ourselves as a policeman who is handcuffing the thoughts, and bringing them to Jesus.

One of the ways to check for fear in our life, is to ask ourselves this question: "What is the worst thing that could happen in my life?"

Whatever our answer is, is probably something we fear.

Example prayer:

Lord, I take responsibility and repent for allowing fear to operate in my life.

Lord, please remove all the fear from me, especially the fear of _____ (name the fears) _____ and I ask for the blood of Jesus to wash them away.

Lord, I understand that fear is faith going in the wrong direction.

I now choose to have faith in You, Lord, and trust Your plans for my life.

Lord, please help me to remember to come to You, instead of allowing fear to come to me. Fill me with Your perfect love and peace.

In Jesus Name, Amen.

Blocks to Healing (D-H)

Gossip

Gossip is idle talk or rumors especially about the personal or private affairs of others. It can break down trust and morale and can cause many people to get hurt. It causes reputations to be damaged or destroyed.

In order to gossip, we must harden our heart against the person whom we are speaking about.

We draw a line between ourselves and the other person, and define them as being less than good enough, or we are better than them, and our actions are better than theirs.

Gossip creates a gap between ourselves and God's love. If we go to someone to speak to them about something that we need help with, and we are willing to be helped, and we know they can help us, then it is not gossip.

However, if we speak to somebody about something, and we know they can't help us with it, then it is gossip.

If we speak to someone about our problems, but only for the sake of getting them to agree with our problems, then it is self-pity.

As we harden our heart against more people (or groups of people, etc.), this negativity and feeling of separation will grow and permeate our world.

If this happens, we will find it more and more difficult to access God's love in any aspect of our lives.

Understanding Emotional Healing

To overcome gossiping[96] we need to choose to give people the benefit of the doubt.

We need to take personal responsibility to check out the facts with the person involved.

We can then help them to resolve the situation, instead of passing along information that can hurt people's reputation or future.

Example prayer:

Lord, I take responsibility and repent for all gossip and slander that I allowed to operate in my life.

Lord, I ask that You would apply the blood of Jesus, and cancel the gossip that I allowed to come forth from my mouth.

Lord, please remove it from the spirit realm so that it can't damage or harm the people that it came against.

Lord, I ask that You will heal the people's reputations and their future that was damaged by any gossip that came through me.

Lord, please help me to remember to take personal responsibility to check out the facts with the people involved and help them to resolve the situation, instead of passing along information that can hurt people's reputation or future.

---

[96] Ephesians 5:4 Neither filthiness, nor foolish talking, nor jesting, which are not convenient: but rather giving of thanks.

Blocks to Healing (D-H)

Lord, please help me to remember the power of life and death is in my tongue.

Lord, I choose to speak life and blessings from this day forward.

In Jesus Name, Amen.

Guilt

Guilt occurs when a person has violated a moral standard. It is the state of having committed an offense, crime, violation, or wrong. Is a bad feeling caused by knowing or thinking that we have done something bad or wrong.

Healthy guilt leads to godly sorrow[97]. It is the feeling of responsibility for a mistake or error. It helps us discover where we shouldn't go in life, and what we shouldn't do.

Healthy guilt helps us find our way back towards what's right and repair the torn portions of our life. It reminds us when we don't treat each other well, helping us to avoid sin.

False guilt has nothing to do with what's true and accurate, nor is it related to true repentance. Rather, it is usually the fear of disapproval in disguise. False guilt is a form of self abuse.

False guilt puts heavy burdens upon our backs. Burdens we were never intended to shoulder. When we suffer from false

---

[97] 2 Corinthians 7:10 For godly sorrow worketh repentance to salvation not to be repented of: but the sorrow of the world worketh death.

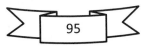

Understanding Emotional Healing

guilt, we will nearly always have difficulty being truthful with how we think, feel, and act.

Healthy guilt is overcome by allowing godly sorrow to lead to repentance. However, false guilt is overcome by confronting the lies and fears and replacing them with truth.

Example prayer:

Lord, I take responsibility and repent for the wrong that I have done. Please restore me back to the moral standard that You have for me. My desire is to do the right thing according to Your plans and purposes for my life.

Lord, please expose the areas in my life where I am believing lies that lead to false guilt. I ask that You would remove those lies from me, and fill me with Your Truth.

Lord, I repent for the insecurity that allows the fear of disapproval to work in my life. Please remove that fear from me and help me to be secure in You. Fill me with Your perfect love that casts out fear[98].

In Jesus Name, Amen.

---

[98] 1 John 4:18 There is no fear in love; but perfect love casteth out fear: because fear hath torment. He that feareth is not made perfect in love.

Blocks to Healing (D-H)

Hopelessness

Hopelessness is not seeing any possibility of a solution. It is believing things are impossible.

Hopelessness is the despair we feel when we have lost hope of ever achieving comfort or success. It is the feeling that everything is wrong, and nothing will turn out right.

Hopelessness comes in when a happening or event breaks our spirit or ability to function. It is the moment we believe that everything in our world is wrong, and there is absolutely nothing we can do about it.

Hopelessness is a feeling that conditions will never improve, and there is no solution to our problem.

Some expressions that people make that come from hopelessness:
- "Things will never get better."
- "There are no solutions to my problems."
- "I will never be happy again."
- "I will never get over what happened."
- "I don't see things ever improving."
- "There is no point in trying anymore."
- "I just want to give up."
- "Things are hopeless."
- "I feel so helpless."
- "There is no hope for me."
- "What do I have to look forward to?"
- "The future is empty for me."

Understanding Emotional Healing

- "I see things getting worse in the future."
- "Everything is going downhill."
- "I will never get back to the way I was."
- "It's too late for me."
- "There is nothing that I can do to make things better."

If we are absolutely convinced that life is hopeless, then we won't do anything to help ourselves. But no matter how hopeless it seems, there are things we can do – right now – that can help us find a way out.

To overcome hopelessness, we need to work on changing our perception and attitude toward the problem. Even though we can't change the circumstances in which we work or live, we can always change our perception and our attitude.

In order to change our perception, we need to start looking at the situation from God's point of view. Is it something that is too much for God? If so, we need a bigger God.

When we focus on our problem being bigger than God, we have no choice but to surrender to the problem. However, when we focus on God being bigger[99] than our problem, then we will have the ability and the opportunity to surrender to God.

Example prayer:

Lord, I take responsibility and repent for not believing that You are big enough to handle my problems.

---

[99] Romans 8:37–39 Nay, in all these things we are more than conquerors through him that loved us. For I am persuaded, that neither death, nor life, nor angels, nor principalities, nor powers, nor things present, nor things to come, nor height, nor depth, nor any other creature, shall be able to separate us from the love of God, which is in Christ Jesus our Lord.

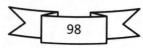

Blocks to Healing (D-H)

Lord, please remove all hopelessness and discouragement from my life and help me see the situation at hand from Your point of view.

*I choose to believe in, and connect to the **HOPE** that You have for me.*

In Jesus Name, Amen.

Understanding Emotional Healing

Chapter 6:
Blocks to Healing
(I-R)

Insecurity

Insecurity is a lack of confidence or assurance. It is self-doubt, lack of stability, and lack of certainty.

Insecurity is a feeling of general unease or nervousness that may be triggered by seeing ourselves as being vulnerable or inferior in some way. It is a feeling of apprehensiveness and uncertainty.

Insecurity is a lack of trust in ourselves or others. It is fearing that a present positive state is temporary, will let us down, and cause us loss or distress.

A person with insecurity lacks confidence in his/her own value and his/her own capabilities.

Understanding Emotional Healing

To overcome insecurity, we need to trust[100] in the Lord with all our heart, and not lean on our own brain (understanding).

Example prayer:

Lord, I take responsibility and repent for not trusting You with all my heart. I repent for allowing insecurity to operate in my life.

Lord, I don't need this insecurity anymore. Please remove it from me, and help me to remember to trust in You.

Lord, I choose to trust You with all my heart, instead of leaning on my brain. Please fill me with Your peace.

Lord, Your Word says that Your strength is made perfect in weakness[101]. I give You my weakness in exchange for Your perfection.

In Jesus Name, Amen.

Insinuations

An insinuation is a sly way of saying something, usually insulting. It is an insult that sneaks in the back door.

---

[100] Proverbs 3:5 Trust in the Lord with all thine heart; and lean not unto thine own understanding.

[101] 2 Corinthians 12:9 And he said unto me, My grace is sufficient for thee: for my strength is made perfect in weakness. Most gladly therefore will I rather glory in my infirmities, that the power of Christ may rest upon me.

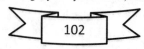

Blocks to Healing (I-R)

An insinuation is an indirect or covert suggestion or hint, especially of a derogatory nature. It is a suggestion, without being direct, that something unpleasant is true.

Insinuations are a roundabout way of trying to communicate something without taking the responsibility of what we are trying to say. It is often motivated by fear of conflict and a fear of being transparent.

To overcome insinuations, we need to take responsibility for our own communication. We need to say what we mean and mean what we say.

Example prayer:

Lord, I repent for not taking responsibility for my own communication. I repent for all the times that I used insinuations to try to communicate instead of being transparent with the person.

Lord, I take authority over all accusations, condemnations, insinuations, and judgments. I bring them to You and ask that You would apply the blood of Jesus to destroy all these curses.

Lord, Your Word says to bless those that curse[102] me, so I ask that You would send blessings to where ever these curses are coming from.

In Jesus Name, Amen.

---

[102] Matthew 5:44 But I say unto you, Love your enemies, bless them that curse you, do good to them that hate you, and pray for them which despitefully use you, and persecute you;

Understanding Emotional Healing

Jealousy

Jealousy is the negative thoughts and feelings of insecurity, fear, and anxiety of the anticipated loss of something of great personal value. It is comparing[103] ourselves to things in the natural realm, and feeling like we come out with the short end of the stick.

Jealousy often consists of anger, resentment, inadequacy, helplessness, and disgust.

Jealousy happens when a person feels that a relationship, that is of importance, is threatened by someone else outside of the relationship.

Jealousy tends to bring out the worst in us, even though we know better. When we are jealous, it usually means we are insecure about something.

Envy and jealousy are often used interchangeably in common usage, but the words stand for two distinct emotions.

Jealousy is the fear of losing someone or something that we are attached to. Envy is the resentment caused by another person having something that we do not have, but we desire it for ourselves.

---

[103] 2 Corinthians 10:12b ...but they measuring themselves by themselves, and comparing themselves among themselves, are not wise.

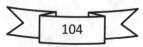

Blocks to Healing (I-R)

Example prayer:

Lord, I take responsibility and repent for allowing envy and jealousy to operate in my life. I repent for comparing myself to others, and what others have.

Lord, please remove all envy and jealousy from my life. I ask for the blood of Jesus to cleanse me from all unrighteousness.

Lord, I choose to be content with the plans that You have for my life. I choose to submit[104] to You, and resist the devil, so that he will flee.

In Jesus Name, Amen.

Judgments

Judgment is a personal belief or decision that is not founded on proof or certainty. It is the act of comparing a person, situation, or event. It is an act of disapproval or condemnation.

Judgments are comparisons, comparing one thing to another, instead of evaluating everything with the cross of Jesus Christ, and the way God sees things.

The Bible says, "Judge not that you be not judged, for with what judgment you judge, you will be judged[105]." Many people

---

[104] James 4:7 Submit yourselves therefore to God. Resist the devil, and he will flee from you.

[105] Matthew 7:1-2 Judge not, that ye be not judged. For with what judgment ye judge, ye shall be judged: and

Understanding Emotional Healing

are judged by the judgments that they judge others with and then they wonder why life is treating them unfairly. These judgments keep them in bondage to their own declarations.

We can quit judging others by evaluating every situation with the Truth. When we cast judgments, we are basing our opinion on what something appears to be.

When we evaluate[106] we take time to gather facts and find the heart of the matter.

Example prayer:

Lord, I take responsibility and repent for all judgments and comparisons, and I ask that You would remove them from my life.

Lord, Your word says that those that compare themselves among themselves are not wise[107]. I ask for wisdom to be released into my life.

Lord, please help me to remember to evaluate the situation instead of judging. I choose to find the heart of the matter and gather facts, instead of comparing and casting judgments.

Lord, I now take authority over all accusations, condemnations, insinuations, and judgments. I bring them to

---

with what measure ye mete, it shall be measured to you again.
[106] John 7:24 Judge not according to the appearance, but judge righteous judgment.
[107] 2 Corinthians 10:12b ...but they measuring themselves by themselves, and comparing themselves among themselves, are not wise.

Blocks to Healing (I-R)

You and ask that You would apply the blood of Jesus to destroy all these curses.

Lord, Your Word says to bless those that curse[108] me, so I ask that You would send blessings to where ever these curses are coming from.

In Jesus Name, Amen.

Lust

Lust is an intense desire of the body that is often confused with love. However, it is purely a physical attraction and has no lasting effect. Lust can be completely unreasonable.

Lust is a willfully allowed pleasurable gratification of wrongfully directed desire (often sexual) that takes place deep inside.

Lust can take on any form, such as the lust for knowledge, the lust for sex, the lust for money, or the lust for power, etc.

When we are 'me' focused, it is not love. It is lust.

Lust will always gratify myself at others' expense. True love will always do things for others at my own expense. That is a good way to measure what we are doing, and why.

---

[108] Matthew 5:44 But I say unto you, Love your enemies, bless them that curse you, do good to them that hate you, and pray for them which despitefully use you, and persecute you;

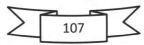

Understanding Emotional Healing

As a little baby, it is expected that we will cry when we are hungry, or when we need to have our needs met. However, as we mature, it is no longer an option to have the 'need to be satisfied' at somebody else's expense.

If we are in a cycle, trying to protect ourselves, it means that we don't trust God. Then we will be looking around to see who will bless me? Who is going to gratify me? Who can endorse me? Who can empower me? God is the one who does this for us.

Lust is looking for love in all the wrong places. If it's not in line with God's will and plans, it is coming from a mindset of victimization and not from love.

The very nature of lust is an unquenchable thirst for more and more. More money, more fame, more power, more revenge, more food, more clothing, more love, etc.

To overcome lust, it is very important to take every thought captive and bring it to the obedience of Christ[109]. Unless our desires are turned over to the Lord, we will never be satisfied.

It is also important to deal with the roots of where the spirit of lust was allowed to enter into our being. When was the first time that I remember lusting?

Perhaps somebody introduced me to pornography, or through defiling conversations, or reading a dirty book, or wrong touch, etc. allowing an evil spirit access to my life.

---

[109] 2 Corinthians 10:5 Casting down imaginations, and every high thing that exalteth itself against the knowledge of God, and bringing into captivity every thought to the obedience of Christ;

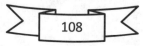

Blocks to Healing (I-R)

It can even be a generational iniquity that was passed on from generation to generation.

Example prayer:

Lord, I take responsibility and repent for looking for gratification in wrongfully directed ways, instead of turning my desires over to You.

Lord, please reveal to me the root of where the lust spirit was allowed to enter into my life. _____ (pause and allow God to reveal the root.)

Lord, I repent for allowing this root to grow in my being. Please remove all the roots of lust from my life. Cleanse[110] and purify my hands, my heart, my mind, and my entire being with the blood of Jesus, and give me the mind of Christ[111].

Lord, I choose to take every thought captive and bring it to the obedience of Christ. Please help me to be 'others' focused instead of 'me' focused. I choose to connect to Your desires for my life, so that I can glorify You in everything I do.

Lord, I choose to do things Your way, use Your power, and use Your knowledge, in Your timing.

In Jesus Name, Amen.

---

[110] James 4:8 Draw nigh to God, and he will draw nigh to you. Cleanse your hands, ye sinners; and purify your hearts, ye double minded.

[111] 1 Corinthians 2:16 For who hath known the mind of the Lord, that he may instruct him? But we have the mind of Christ.

Understanding Emotional Healing

Manipulation

Manipulation is an attempt to change the perception or behavior of others through underhanded, deceptive, or even abusive tactics.

Manipulation is the skillful handling, controlling, or using of something or someone. It can be true or devious management, but it is usually for one's own advantage.

Manipulation can appear to be real and good, however it is the motivation of the heart that determines if it is manipulation, or if it is true Godly influence.

To overcome manipulation, we need to repent to God for selfish ambitions and motivations. We need to make a decision to make God first in our life, and point people to God instead of insisting on having our own way.

Example prayer:

Lord, I take responsibility and repent for all the times that I used manipulation to have my own way.

Lord, I repent for not preferring[112] my fellow man according to Your plans.

Please remove all the manipulation from my life, and help me to be a true Godly influence.

In Jesus Name, Amen.

---

[112] Romans 12:10 Be kindly affectioned one to another with brotherly love; in honour preferring one another;

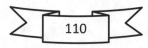

Blocks to Healing (I-R)

Offenses

Offenses need to be looked at both from the giving side and the receiving side. Offenses that we inflict on others need to be repented of. Offenses that others inflict upon us need to be forgiven.

Offenses are feelings of woundedness, and come from a failure to show regard for others. It produces the effect of deliberate disrespect. It is the act of displeasing or affronting.

Offenses arouse serious negative emotions in people who believe they have been wronged, and are often a stumbling block which can cause the state of being insulted or morally outraged.

We believe that a Christian should never be able to be offended. If we ever get offended it means that something needs to be healed in that area of our heart. As we surrender our heart to the Lord, He will heal the offenses[113] that come against us.

The Bible tells us that with the shield of faith we can quench **ALL** the fiery darts[114] of the wicked one. If a fiery dart ever gets through, it means that our shield of faith was not used properly.

Every day of our life there are opportunities to take offense at things. Only when we receive the offenses, do they have any power to control or damage our lives.

---

[113] Romans 4:25 Who was delivered for our offences, and was raised again for our justification.

[114] Ephesians 6:16 Above all, taking the shield of faith, wherewith ye shall be able to quench all the fiery darts of the wicked.

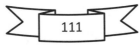

Understanding Emotional Healing

When offenses come we have an opportunity to give them directly to the Lord instead of receiving them.

Example prayer:

Lord, I take responsibility and repent for all the offenses that I have received from others. I choose to forgive them and turn the offenses over to You, Lord.

Lord, I also repent for all the offenses that have caused others to stumble. Please remove all the effects from the projected offenses that others received from me, and heal the people who have been offended by me.

*Lord, help me to remember to use the shield of faith that will quench **ALL** the fiery darts of the wicked one.*

In Jesus Name, Amen.

Performance

Performance is the undertaking of a duty, an achievement, a deed, an act, a job, etc.

Performance in itself is not wrong. However, many people are pressured to perform.

Many people have a problem seeing who they really are. This causes an unhealthy need to look to others for acceptance and approval.

Blocks to Healing (I-R)

When a person looks to others for acceptance and approval instead of looking to God, they will be controlled by the other person's opinions.

If someone does not know who they really are in Jesus Christ, they tend to have fear of man or an unhealthy need for approval by others. This can cause a spirit of performance to operate in their life.

When the spirit of performance is at work, it is difficult to relax and do things God's way.

When we operate under a spirit of performance[115] it will rob our peace. True peace will only be available to us when we connect to who God says we are.

When we align to who God says we are, we will perform **because** of who we are, instead of trying to **be** who we already are.

Example prayer:

Lord, I forgive everyone in my life who has not accepted me for who I am. I take responsibility and repent for allowing a spirit of performance to operate in my life.

Lord, I now choose to align with who You say that I am. I choose to flow with Your plans and purposes for my life, instead of focusing on who other people think I should be.

---

[115] Luke 10:40-41 But Martha was cumbered about much serving, and came to him, and said, Lord, dost thou not care that my sister has left me to serve alone? bid her therefore that she help me. And Jesus answered and said unto her, Martha, Martha, thou art careful and troubled about many things:

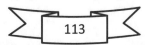

Understanding Emotional Healing

Lord, please help me to trust You with all my heart[116], and not lean on my own understanding.

In Jesus Name, Amen.

Pride

Pride is the frame of mind in which a person, through the love of his own worth, aims to withdraw himself from subjection to Almighty God. It is anything we believe that is contrary to God's word.

Pride is a high or exalted opinion of our own dignity, importance, merit, or superiority. It is the excessive love of our own excellence. Pride is the only cause of contention[117].

False humility is also a form of pride, because it is exalting[118] ourselves against the knowledge of God. It is saying that we are less than what God says we are.

For example, degrading ourselves and denying or discounting our gifts and abilities.

When we wallow around in a pit of misery and despair, we are extremely proud and we are refusing to humble[119] ourselves before God.

---

[116] Proverbs 3:5 Trust in the Lord with all thine heart; and lean not unto thine own understanding.

[117] Proverbs 13:10 Only by pride cometh contention: but with the well advised is wisdom.

[118] 2 Corinthians 10:5 Casting down imaginations, and every high thing that exalteth itself against the knowledge of God, and bringing into captivity every thought to the obedience of Christ;

[119] 1 Peter 5:6 Humble yourselves therefore under the mighty hand of God, that he may exalt you in due time:

Blocks to Healing (I-R)

Because we are not open to hearing the truth, we will be living under a spirit of accusation that is bringing condemnation[120] into our lives. The only way to get free from this pit is to hear the truth without condemnation.

True humility is agreeing with exactly who God says we are, and agreeing with what God says we can do (no more and no less).

Many people give away their authority by trying to be humble, but they have no idea what true humility is, and they come into agreement with the enemy by coming into false humility, which is pride.

The enemy is still trying to trick us in the same way he tricked Adam and Eve in the Garden of Eden. The devil implied to them that God was holding something back from them and was not giving them His best. The devil tricked them into believing that eating from the tree of knowledge of good and evil was beneficial[121] to them.

Eating from the tree of the knowledge of good and evil is the result of the need to understand things before obedience and faith. But the truth of the matter is, when they ate of the tree of the knowledge of good and evil, they were cut off from the Tree of Life which is the true connection to God.

---

[120] Romans 8:1 There is therefore now no condemnation to them which are in Christ Jesus, who walk not after the flesh, but after the Spirit.

[121] Genesis 3:6 And when the woman saw that the tree was good for food, and that it was pleasant to the eyes, and a tree to be desired to make one wise, she took of the fruit thereof, and did eat, and gave also unto her husband with her; and he did eat.

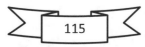

Understanding Emotional Healing

To overcome pride we need to, first of all, submit[122] ourselves completely to God. Then we need to come into agreement with exactly who[123] God says we are, and believe that we can do[124] exactly what He says that we can do, go[125] where He says to go, and be[126] who He says to be.

Example prayer:

Lord, I take responsibility and repent for all forms of pride that I allowed to operate in my life. I repent for exalting myself above the knowledge of God.

Lord, I also repent for allowing false humility to operate in my life, by agreeing with the enemy, when he says that I am less than what God says I am.

Lord, I repent for believing that my problems are too big for You to handle. I choose to humble myself before You and trust you.

Lord, I choose to walk in the authority that You have given me, and to do no more and no less than what You are showing me to do.

---

[122] James 4:7 Submit yourselves therefore to God. Resist the devil, and he will flee from you.

[123] Romans 8:15 For ye have not received the spirit of bondage again to fear; but ye have received the Spirit of adoption, whereby we cry, Abba, Father.

[124] Philippians 4:13 I can do all things through Christ which strengtheneth me.

[125] Mark 16:15 And he said unto them, Go ye into all the world, and preach the gospel to every creature.

[126] 2 Corinthians 5:20 Now then we are ambassadors for Christ, as though God did beseech you by us: we pray you in Christ's stead, be ye reconciled to God.

Blocks to Healing (I-R)

Lord, please help me to remember to agree with, and be obedient to Your Truth.

In Jesus Name, Amen.

Rebellion

Rebellion is an act or show of defiance against true Godly authority[127]. It is the refusal of obedience or alliance to the plans and purposes of God's principles.

Rebellion is an opposition against a person or group in authority. It is a refusal to flow with the agreements and the direction of the corporate vision. It is opposition to one in authority or dominance.

A person operating in rebellion will find it almost impossible to do what they are asked to do. Even simple requests or suggestions are hard for them to carry out without changing something about it in order to make it their own thing.

It is impossible to overcome rebellion without making a choice to submit to God, and to the people in authority.

Many times people in the position of authority are not walking with God, which makes it difficult to submit to them. When people are in the position of authority in our life, we need to walk in their authority wherever they are submitted to God.

---

[127] Romans 13:1-2 Let every soul be subject unto the higher powers. For there is no power but of God: the powers that be are ordained of God. Whosoever therefore resisteth the power, resisteth the ordinance of God: and they that resist shall receive to themselves damnation.

Understanding Emotional Healing

If people in authority are not submitted to God, it is our responsibility to pray for them, and to submit the best that we can without compromising God's principles for our life.

We can then cover their backs, and stand in the gap against the spirits that are working through them that are not from God.

Example prayer:

Lord, I take responsibility and repent for all forms of rebellion that I allowed to operate in my life. Please remove the spirit of rebellion and any witchcraft[128] connected to it.

Lord, I choose to submit to You, and to the authority that You have placed in my life.

Lord, please help me submit the best I can without compromising Your principles for my life.

Lord, I choose to pray for the people in authority, and to stand in the gap for them in the areas that the enemy is deceiving them.

Lord, please help me to walk in true humility, and to respect the authority that I am connected to.

In Jesus Name, Amen.

---

[128] 1 Samuel 15:23 For rebellion is as the sin of witchcraft, and stubbornness is as iniquity and idolatry. Because thou hast rejected thee word of the LORD, he has also rejected the from being king.

Blocks to Healing (I-R)

Rejection

Rejection is the act of being cut off from something or someone. It can refer to the actual act of rejecting something or someone, or to the feeling one has after being rejected.

Many people are going through life and have no real concept of who they really are. Because of being compared to others, they may be trying to be who others want them to be, so they won't get rejected.

If they are trying to be somebody else, they have to reject themselves in order to function in the fakeness.

Many people, as very little children, start to step out in the gifts that God has given them. However, the way they go about expressing themselves, and speaking truth about situations that people are trying to hide or keep hidden, is often rejected. This can cause a spirit of rejection to come upon the child at an early age.

With limited knowledge, we, as little children may have blocked off our heart to protect ourselves from being hurt.

When we do that we block off our true identity which also blocks us off from trusting God and distorts our gifts. We then begin to take on a false identity, and try to be like somebody else, so we don't feel the rejection.

By taking on a false identity so we don't feel rejection, we are actually rejecting our true self. This is rejection of who we really

Understanding Emotional Healing

are, and by doing this we have no basis of being real with ourselves, others, or God.

To get free from this bondage, we need to understand who we are in Christ. If we have never accepted Jesus Christ as our Savior **AND LORD**, it is impossible to get free from rejection.

When Jesus Christ is our Lord, we will be who He called us to be, do what He asks us to do, and go where He asks us to go. We need to accept the destiny, the plans, and the purposes that God has planned for our life.

We need to take **all** thoughts and feelings captive (the good and the bad ones), and bring them to the obedience of Christ.

We need to stand, and above all stand, in who God says we are.

Example prayer:

Lord, I forgive everyone who has ever hurt me, misused me, mistreated me, abused me, abandoned me, rejected me, or who wasn't there for me when I needed them. It doesn't mean what they did was right, it just means that I choose to trust You and give it to You, Lord, and I forgive them.

*Lord, Your Word says to bless[129] those that curse me, so I choose to bless **ALL** the people who have transgressed against me.*

---

[129] Matthew 5:44 But I say unto you, Love your enemies, bless them that curse you, do good to them that hate you, and pray for them which despitefully use you, and persecute you;

Blocks to Healing (I-R)

And Lord, I forgive myself for every mistake that I have ever made, and I choose to receive the forgiveness that You have for me.

Lord, I ask that You would hold me in Your arms, protect me, love me, and heal me.

Lord, I also repent for blocking off my heart and rejecting myself.

Lord, please remove the spirit of rejection from my life, and help me to accept who You have called me to be.

In Jesus Name, Amen.

Resentment

Resentment is the feeling of displeasure or indignation at some action, remark, or person, regarded as causing injury or insult. It is the strong and painful bitterness we feel when we believe someone did something wrong to us.

Resentment can come from doing things to please others, instead of doing what we believe is the right thing to do.

Regret can surface when we do things to please others that we would normally not do, but we are only doing it to satisfy them.

We then begin to secretly hold it against that person. We may, or may not, take it out on them, but it begins to eat us up on the inside.

Understanding Emotional Healing

Resentment often functions in a downward spiral. Resentful feelings often cut off communication between the resentful person and the person they feel committed the offense.

This can result in future mis-communications, and the development of further resentful feelings.

Resentment usually occurs after the injury has already been received, and after the offended person has had some time to think about it.

Resentment is a very personal and private emotion, and has almost no effect on a person it is directed towards. It can cause extreme negativity and pain.

Our resentment tends to punish our family and friends, because they will feel a need to tiptoe around our resentment.

This can cause them to feel like they need to walk around on eggshells when they are around us. This, in turn, can cause them to tend to want to leave us alone, which can cause us much loneliness.

The way to overcome resentment is by going to God, and asking Him to be in charge of our justice. We've been hurt and we want justice, but that is His job, not ours.

He is the One who makes things right. When we return that responsibility to God, we will feel a heavy load[130] come off our back.

---

[130] Matthew 11:30 For my yoke is easy, and my burden is light.

Blocks to Healing (I-R)

When we remember that resentment is a choice, then we will learn to choose peace and contentment[131] instead.

<u>Example prayer:</u>

Lord, I take responsibility and repent for all the resentment, bitterness, and offenses, that I have carried in my heart.

Lord, I ask that You would remove the root of bitterness and resentment from my life, and that You would heal the people who have been defiled by my bitterness and resentment.

Lord, I choose to forgive and bless the people in every situation who have offended me.

Lord, I ask that you would cleanse my heart from all unrighteousness, and purify my life. I now choose peace and contentment for my life.

In Jesus Name, Amen.

Retaliation

Retaliation is doing something bad to someone who has hurt us or treated us badly. It is an act of revenge by the infliction of equal or greater injuries than were received.

---

[131] 1 Timothy 6:6 But godliness with contentment is great gain.

Understanding Emotional Healing

Retaliation is returning evil for evil[132]. It may be a violent or a subtle response to an act of harm or perceived injustice.

Many people use the spirit of retaliation to survive because they don't trust God[133] to deal with the situations as they come up.

If we can release all the injustices to God, we give the responsibility back to Him, and He will deal with the situations.

Many people do not feel God's protection which can tempt them to feel like they have to protect themselves.

When we believe we need to protect ourselves we will fight back in the natural realm, which is a very weak attempt to work out and deal with our own perceived injustices.

When we know who we are in Christ we will know that we can do all things[134] through Christ who strengthens us.

We are more than[135] conquerors through Jesus Christ, and we also know that all things will work[136] out for good for those who love God and are called according to His purposes.

---

[132] Matthew 5:38-39 Ye have heard that it hath been said, An eye for an eye, and a tooth for a tooth: But I say unto you, That you resist not evil: but whosoever shall smite thee on thy right cheek, turn to him the other also.

[133] Romans 12:19 Dearly beloved, avenge not yourselves, but rather give place unto wrath: for it is written, Vengeance is mine; I will repay, saith the Lord.

[134] Philippians 4:13 I can do all things through Christ which strengtheneth me.

[135] Romans 8:37 Nay, in all of these things we are more than conquerors through him that loved us.

[136] Romans 8:28 And we know that all things work together for good to them that love God, to them who are the called according to his purpose.

Blocks to Healing (I-R)

To effectively fight the battle in the spirit realm, we need to put on the armor of light[137], which is the whole armor[138] of God.

It is important for us to remember that we are not wrestling with flesh and blood (we recognize that we are not fighting against each other), but we wrestle[139] against principalities, and powers, and the rulers of the darkness of this world, and spiritual wickedness in high places.

For our true Godly protection, we need to put on the whole armor of God, which is the helmet of salvation, the breastplate of righteousness, loins girt about with truth, our feet shod with the preparation of the gospel of peace, the shield of faith that will quench all the fiery darts of the wicked one[140], and the sword of the Spirit which is the Word of God.

When we trust in the Lord with all our heart[141], and lean not on our own understanding, we can walk with God into any situation that He has called us to, and not worry about being unprotected.

We also know that God has not given us a spirit of fear, but

---

[137] Romans 13:12 The night is far spent, the day is at hand: let us therefore cast off the works of darkness, and let us put on the armour of light.

[138] Ephesians 6:13 Wherefore take unto you the whole armour of God, that ye may be able to withstand in the evil day, and having done all, to stand.

[139] Ephesians 6:12 For we wrestle not against flesh and blood, but against principalities, against powers, against the rulers of the darkness of this world, against spiritual wickedness in high places.

[140] Ephesians 6:14-17 Stand therefore, having your loins girt about with truth, and having on the breastplate of righteousness; And your feet shod with the preparation of the gospel of peace; Above all, taking the shield of faith, wherewith ye shall be able to quench all the fiery darts of the wicked. And take the helmet of salvation, and the sword of the Spirit, which is the word of God:

[141] Proverbs 3:5-6 Trust in the LORD with all thine heart; and lean not unto thine own understanding. In all thy ways acknowledge him, and he shall direct thy paths

Understanding Emotional Healing

of power, love, and a sound mind[142]. Perfect love is a powerful weapon that we can use against the enemy to cast out fear[143].

When we don't have fear, we have power, we have love, and we have a sound mind. With power, love, and a sound mind, nothing can stop us.

Example prayer:

Lord, I forgive everyone who has ever hurt me, misused me, mistreated me, abused me, abandoned me, rejected me, or who wasn't there for me when I needed them. It doesn't mean what they did was right, it just means that I choose to trust You and give it to You, Lord, and I forgive them.

*Lord, Your Word says to bless[144] those that curse me, so I choose to bless **ALL** the people who have transgressed against me.*

And Lord, I forgive myself for every mistake that I have ever made, and I choose to receive the forgiveness that You have for me.

Lord, I ask that You would hold me in Your arms, protect me, love me, and heal me.

---

[142] 2 Timothy 1:7 For God has not given us the spirit of fear; but of power, and of love, and of a sound mind.

[143] 1 John 4:18 There is no fear in love; but perfect love casteth out fear: because fear hath torment. He that fear is is not made perfect in love.

[144] Matthew 5:44 But I say unto you, Love your enemies, bless them that curse you, do good to them that hate you, and pray for them which despitefully use you, and persecute you;

Blocks to Healing (I-R)

Lord, I also repent for blocking off my heart and resenting others.

Lord, please remove the spirit of retaliation from my life, and help me to trust You to protect me.

In Jesus Name, Amen.

Understanding Emotional Healing

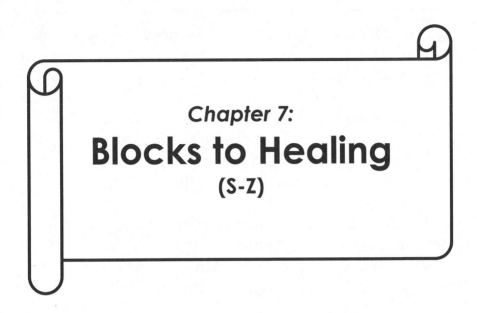

Chapter 7:
Blocks to Healing
(S-Z)

Self-Pity

Self-pity is the state of mind of an individual who has not accepted the adverse situation that they perceive they are in. It is the person's belief that they are a victim of unfortunate circumstances or events, and are therefore deserving of comfort.

Self-pity is a feeling of pity for ourselves because we believe we have suffered more than is fair or reasonable. It comes from believing that we are the victim who has done no wrong, and is therefore deserving comfort from everyone else.

Self-pity is like an icky liquid we swim around in when we blame the world for our problems. If we wallow around in self-pity, we will usually go around in a bad mood, feeling sorry for ourselves, and feeling we have been wronged somehow.

Understanding Emotional Healing

We only care about poor little me. We believe we have failed because of someone or something else. We don't own up to our own faults and weaknesses.

Self-pity is a manipulative tool that people use to control situations etc. If we speak to someone about our problems, but only for the reason to get them to agree with our problems, instead of finding a solution, then it is self-pity.

The truth of the matter is, God cares about our hurts, but He doesn't want us to be in control of the problems. God wants us to trust Him with all of our problems. Many people believe if they don't step in and do something about it, God will let them down.

To overcome self-pity, we need to realize that God does care about our situation, and He is willing to help us. We need to focus on the things that God is focusing on.

It will not work to focus on our big problems with a little god, but rather to focus on Almighty God who is able to handle every problem.

To help others overcome self-pity, we can listen to their story, and then help them to take their problems and challenges to the cross of Jesus Christ to be resolved.

We need to be careful that we do not fall into the trap of agreeing with their gripes and offenses. When we agree with their gripes and offenses, we will be adding to the problem, instead of helping to bring a solution to the situation.

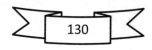

Blocks to Healing (S-Z)

Example prayer:

Lord, I take responsibility and repent for all the self-pity, bitterness, and offenses, that I have carried in my heart.

Lord, I ask that You would remove the root of bitterness and self-pity from my life, and that You would heal the people who have been bogged down by my self-pity and defiled by my bitterness.

Lord, I choose to stand in the authority that You have given me, and I take responsibility for my life. I recognize that I don't have to hold on to self-pity anymore.

Lord, I now take the opportunity and repent for what is my part, and I forgive the others for what they have done against me.

Lord, I choose to forgive and bless the people in every situation who have offended me, and I choose to let go of all self-pity.

Lord, I ask that you would cleanse my heart from all unrighteousness, and purify my life. I now choose peace and contentment for my life.

In Jesus Name, Amen.

Understanding Emotional Healing

Selfishness

Selfishness is when we show concern only for ourselves, and not for the needs or feelings of other people. It is when we concentrate on having things to our own advantage, pleasure, or well-being without regard to others.

Selfishness is the condition of putting our own interests before those of others. It causes stinginess because we think only about ourselves and what we want.

When we are selfish, we will end up losing our friends or loved ones, because no matter how charming or interesting a selfish person may be, a relationship with a selfish person is very hard to maintain.

A truly selfish person would never consider the possibility that they are selfish. Many think selfishness and pride are good things, and that putting the needs of others above our own is for suckers.

To overcome selfishness we need to realize that it is a work of the flesh. To be truly empowered, we will give our life to Jesus Christ, and we will be dedicated to His plans and purposes.

We also will work with other people to help them fulfill their plans and purposes for a greater cause.

One of the enemy's objectives is to get us divided. If an enemy can divide us, it is easier to conquer us. If we can see the truth, we will know that we are all in this together against the enemy.

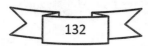

Blocks to Healing (S-Z)

When we can let go of selfishness, we can come together as one, in the unity of the Spirit. When we come together in the unity of the Spirit, we will focus on the greater picture.

God has a big plan for our lives and for the lives of others. The only way to fulfill God's plan is for us to realize that we are placed on 'one team' with God.

Because we are on God's team, we will be able to withstand all the plans that the enemy sends against us to cause us to stumble.

A selfish person has given up on God, and decided that it is better to take matters into his/her own hands. They will not have the concept or the benefits of being a team participant.

We need to work as a team so we can accomplish what God has ordained for us to accomplish together.

Example prayer:

Lord, I take responsibility and repent for all forms of selfishness and pride that I allowed to operate in my life. I repent for exalting myself above the knowledge of God.

Lord, I repent for believing that I can handle my own problems without You. I choose to humble myself before You and trust you.

Lord, please teach me how to be a team participant to do Your will instead of trying to do my own things.

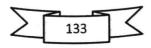

Understanding Emotional Healing

Lord, I choose to walk in the authority that You have given me, and to do no more and no less than what You are showing me to do.

Lord, please help me to remember to agree with, and be obedient to Your Truth.

In Jesus Name, Amen.

Sex (Unholy)

Unholy sex includes any form of sex that is not sanctioned by God. This includes all forms of sexual immorality.

Sexual immorality is caused by violating the principles and the plans that God has for true intimacy.

Sexual immorality happens when people focus on their own fleshly desires and lusts[145] in the natural realm, instead of having true intimacy with God in the spiritual realm. They do not honor and glorify[146] God as being the Sovereign Lord of the Truth.

Sexual immorality is a result of compromise[147]. When people compromise God's truth, it opens themselves, their descendants,

---

[145] Romans 1:24 Wherefore God also gave them up to uncleanness through the lusts of their own hearts, to dishonour their own bodies between themselves:

[146] Romans 1:21-22 Because that, when they knew God, they glorified him not as God, neither were thankful; but became vain in their imaginations, and their foolish heart was darkened. Professing themselves to be wise, they became fools,

[147] Revelations 2:14 But I have a few things against thee, because thou hast therefore them that hold the doctrine of Balaam, who taught Balac to cast a stumbling block before the children of Israel, to eat things sacrificed unto idols, and to commit fornication.

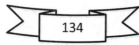

Blocks to Healing (S-Z)

and their people group to a false intimacy which allows sexual immorality to become a stronghold. By compromising God's truth, they are actually rejecting the knowledge[148] of God.

Sexual immorality includes but is not limited to:
- Sex outside of marriage
- Adultery
- Sexual immorality within marriage
- Masturbation
- Pornography
- Immodesty
- Homosexuality
- Incest
- Bestiality

Sexual immorality is a counterfeit supplied by the enemy to try to derail God's plan for deep relationships. To have a deep relationship with God and others, it is necessary to open up the heart.

Many people are unwilling to face the wounds of the heart, and therefore they try to live in denial, and begin to love the wages of unrighteousness[149].

The wages of unrighteousness is short-term pleasure for long term pain. The wages of righteousness is short-term pain for long-term pleasure.

---

[148] Hosea 4:6 My people are destroyed for lack of knowledge: because thou hast rejected knowledge, I will also reject thee, that thou shalt be no priest to me: seeing thou hast forgotten the law of thy God, I will also forget thy children.

[149] 2 Peter 2:15 Which have forsaken the right way, and are gone astray, following the way of Balaam the son of Bosor, who loved the wages of unrighteousness;

Understanding Emotional Healing

Sexual immorality is used by the enemy to bring confusion and compromise in the lives of little children through abuse. This will cause them to have a difficulty to trust in God.

Sexual abuse directed at small children will cause them to lose their voice, will cause them to feel alone, neglected, abandoned, and will cause wounds in their soul. When they grow up, these soul wounds will mess up their marriage, if they are not taken care of.

With wounds in their souls, people will go around looking for love in all the wrong places, driven by a spirit of lust. Sexual immorality is a performance-based plan of the enemy to keep people from being free.

This is one of the deepest ways that the enemy is messing up people, because it is a perversion of the true intimacy that God designed us for.

The enemy is using this to advance the kingdom of darkness by creating more hurts, which makes people react. Jesus wants to advance the Kingdom of God by creating a safe place that is protected and secure in the love and intimacy of God.

If true intimacy is lacking in our lives, we will never be free.

Example prayer:

Lord, I take responsibility and repent for my sins, the sins of my forefathers, the sins of my people, and the sins of our nation.

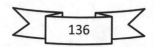

Blocks to Healing (S-Z)

Lord, I also repent for all forms of sexual immorality including _____(name the sin)_____ and I repent for the compromise that opened the door for this sexual immorality to gain access in our lives.

I also repent on behalf of the church, for the areas where the church has compromised instead of standing for Truth.

Lord, I ask that You would awaken the church, bring conviction, restore righteousness and purity, and activate a passion for advancing the Kingdom of God here on earth[150] as in Heaven.

Lord, I repent on behalf of the government, for allowing compromise to open the door to homosexuality and other sexual immorality.

I ask, Lord, that You would break and destroy the curse of these sins and iniquities, and restore us to righteousness.

In Jesus Name, Amen.

Sex (Withheld)

When a man and woman get married, they make a commitment to each other.

This commitment is a covenant stating they are committed to each other 'for better or for worse, for richer or for poorer, in

---

[150] Matthew 6:10 Thy kingdom come. Thy will be done in earth, as it is in heaven.

Understanding Emotional Healing

good times and in bad times, in sickness and in health, until death do us part'.

When this level of commitment is made between husband and wife, it is now expected that they have an intimate relationship that is completely transparent. At this point we are now committed to our spouse and we are no longer in charge[151] of our own life.

To withhold deep intimate sexual relationships from a spouse at this point has the potential to damage relationships. This will create an open door for the enemy to come in and manipulate and put wedges between husband and wife.

To overcome this manipulation and these wedges, the husband and wife need to come into agreement with who God says they are. They need to respect each other, and recommit to surrender their life to each other.

Sex should never be withheld in a marriage unless both the husband and the wife agree to a time of prayer and fasting[152].

If they are not fasting during this time, it allows the enemy a foothold to work at destroying their marriage.

If prayer and fasting does not resolve the situation, it may be helpful to search deeper to find the root of the issues that are keeping God's Divine flow from manifesting in their marriage.

---

[151] 1 Corinthians 7:4 The wife hath not power of her own body, but the husband: and likewise also the husband hath not power of his own body, but the wife.

[152] 1 Corinthians 7:5 Defraud ye not one the other, except it be with consent for a time, that ye may give yourselves to fasting and prayer; and come together again, that satan tempt you not for your incontinency.

Blocks to Healing (S-Z)

Many times when a couple has a hard time trusting each other, we find that there was an impure relationship with each other, or with others, before their marriage.

When they repent before God and to each other, and are completely open and honest with each other, and share their hearts with each other, they will find that trust begins to build again.

Example prayer:

Lord, I take responsibility and repent for withholding sexual intimacy from my spouse. I also repent for every way that I used sex or withheld sex to manipulate or to control my spouse.

Lord, I recognize that by withholding sex I was allowing the enemy to gain a foothold at destroying our marriage.

Lord, I repent for not fasting and praying during the time that my spouse and I were not sexually in agreement with each other.

Lord, I now choose to dedicate my marriage to You and to do things Your way.

In Jesus Name, Amen.

Shame

Shame is the painful feeling arising from the consciousness of

Understanding Emotional Healing

something dishonorable, disgraceful, or improper that was done by one's self or by someone else.

Shame is the feeling of guilt, regret, unworthiness, or sadness that we have because we know that we have done something wrong.

Living with shame is a suffocating feeling. It is like having a blanket over our head and pulled in tightly around our neck.

Example prayer:

Lord, I take responsibility and repent for the wrong that I have done. I also forgive the others for what they have done against me.

Lord, please remove the shame and restore me back to the standard of glory and honor[153] that You have for me. My desire is to do the right thing according to Your plans and purposes for my life.

Lord, please expose the areas in my life where I am believing lies that lead to false guilt and shame.

Lord, I ask that You would remove those lies from me, and fill me with Your Truth.

Lord, I repent for the insecurity that allows the fear of disapproval to work in my life. Please remove that fear from

---

[153] Hebrews 2:6-7 But one in a certain place testified, saying, What is man, that thou art mindful of him? or the son of man, that thou visitest him? Now madest him a little lower than the angels; thou crownedest him with glory and honour, and didst set him over the works of thy hands:

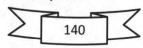

Blocks to Healing (S-Z)

me and help me to be secure in You. Fill me with Your perfect love that cast out fear[154].

In Jesus Name, Amen.

Soul Ties

Soul ties can serve many functions, but in the simplest form, it ties two or more sources together in the spiritual realm.

Soul ties between married couples draw them together like magnets. Soul ties between fornicators can draw a beaten and abused woman to the man, which in the natural realm she would hate and run from. Instead she runs to him, even though he doesn't love her, and treats her like dirt.

In the demonic world, unholy soul ties can serve as bridges between two people, keeping an unhealthy connection between the perpetrator and the abused.

Soul ties can allow a person to manipulate and control another person. The other person may be unaware of what is going on, but for some unknown reason, allows it to continue.

Soul ties are formed through sexual relations, close relationships, vows, oaths, commitments, and agreements.

Unholy sex is one of the most common ways for ungodly soul ties to be created. These soul ties can also be held together, or

---

[154] 1 John 4:18 There is no fear in love; but perfect love casteth out fear: because fear hath torment. He that feareth is not made perfect in love.

Understanding Emotional Healing

strengthened, by gifts that were given, such as rings, flowers, cards, etc.

Any vows or commitments made during fornication need to be renounced and repented of. Even things like "I will love you forever", or "I could never love another person the way I love you" need to be repented of and renounced. They need to be undone verbally because they were spoken commitments.

Example prayer:

Lord, I take responsibility and repent for every ungodly soul tie that was formed between myself and _____ (name the person)_____ as a result of _____ (name the sin)_____ .

Lord, I renounce the ungodly soul tie and in the name of Jesus, I now break and cut off every ungodly soul tie that was formed in this connection between myself and _____ (name the person)_____ .

Lord I ask that you would return to me any pieces of my soul that I transferred to _____ (name the person)_____ and I give back any pieces of their soul that I was hanging on to.

Lord, I now choose to connect my soul to You, and to the people that You have connected me to.

Lord, I declare that from this day forward I will only have

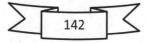

Blocks to Healing (S-Z)

Godly soul ties in my life, and every soul tie that I have must be Godly, or it must leave my presence right now.

In Jesus Name, Amen.

Stress

Stress is the result of the heart and the mind not being in agreement with each other. When the heart and the mind are not in agreement, the heart will always end up winning in the end.

It is impossible to have stress when we are fully trusting the Lord with our problems. If we have stress, it is important to find what is blocking the Divine flow of God from flowing in our life.

When people are in self rejection, the mind will get one picture and the heart will get a different picture. It is necessary to get rid of self rejection, so that the heart and the mind can align and work together.

For us to function properly, the heart needs to function like the engine and the mind needs to function like the transmission.

Example prayer:

Lord, I recognize that I have stress in my life caused by my mind and my heart not being in agreement. I repent for closing down my heart and rejecting myself.

Lord, I forgive myself for every mistake that I have ever made, and I choose to receive the forgiveness that You have for me.

Understanding Emotional Healing

Lord, please remove the spirit of rejection from my life, and help me to accept who You have called me to be.

I now choose to have faith in You, Lord, and trust Your plans for my life.

In Jesus Name, Amen.

Unbelief

Unbelief is the lack of faith in the promises of God. It comes from doubting God's willingness, or ability, to alter the circumstances that we are in.

Unbelief comes from refusing to accept anything which we do not understand. It is refusing to admit the truth of God's revealed Word.

Unbelief is intellectually reconsidering whether or not something we are believing for, can or will occur. It is doubting God's ability to fulfill His Word.

Unbelief can be a progressive process moving from uncertainty, to doubt, to unbelief. We might start out believing, but after a period of time passes without a fulfillment of what we are believing for, we allow discouragement to come in, which leads to unbelief.

Unbelief first manifested in the garden, when the serpent came to Eve and said, "Has God really said…?"

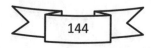

Blocks to Healing (S-Z)

The cure for unbelief[155] is obedience to God. It is making a firm decision on what we believe, and then sticking to it during the hard times.

Without faith it is impossible[156] to please God.

Example prayer:

Lord, I take responsibility and repent for all unbelief that I allowed to operate in my life. I repent for not believing the promises that You have for me.

Lord, I repent for being disobedient to Your Word, and for needing to understand everything before I believe.

Lord, I repent for believing that You are not willing, or able to, handle my situation. I repent for doubting that You have my best interest in mind.

Lord, I choose to believe that You know what You are doing, and that You have everything under control.

I choose to submit to You, Lord, and I choose to resist the enemy.

In Jesus Name, Amen.

---

[155] Hebrews 3:12 Take heed, brethren, lest there be in any of you an evil heart of unbelief, in departing from the living God.

[156] Hebrews 11:6 But without faith it is impossible to please him: for he that cometh to God must believe that he is, and that he is a rewarder of them that diligently seek him.

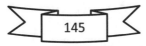

Understanding Emotional Healing

Unforgiveness

Unforgiveness is the unwillingness to give up our resentment towards someone who has wronged us, regardless of how serious or painful that wrong might have been.

Unforgiveness is a conscious decision to resent the wrong and the wrongdoer, and to seek revenge. It is often associated with bitterness, wrath, anger, slander, and malice[157].

Unforgiveness is a self-imposed bondage. It is a grudge against someone who has offended us, and will keep us from being the person God wants us to be. It will prevent us from carrying out God's will for our life.

Unforgiveness is an act of pride, rebellion, and deliberate disobedience to the Word of God. The Bible tells us if we do not forgive, our Father in Heaven will not forgive our trespasses[158].

An unforgiving heart clings to the past, refusing to extend to others what God has extended to us. One of the most significant repercussions of unforgiveness is bitterness[159], which takes root in the heart, and it spreads its poison to choke out every Godly trait there.

Many people are unwilling to forgive because they believe the other person needs to change before they deserve forgiveness.

---

[157] Ephesians 4:31 Let all bitterness, and wrath, and anger, and clamour, and evil speaking, be put away from you, with all malice:

[158] Matthew 6:15 But if ye forgive not men their trespasses, neither will your Father forgive your trespasses.

[159] Hebrews 12:15 Looking diligently lest and a man fail of the grace of God; lest any root of bitterness springing up trouble you, and thereby many be defiled;

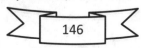

Blocks to Healing (S-Z)

However, unforgiveness does not hurt the other person, it only hurts us. Holding unforgiveness against someone is like drinking poison and hoping the other person gets sick.

Unforgiveness is like a rope that is connected between us and the other person. When we are willing to forgive, we can give our end of the rope to God, and allow Him to deal with the situation.

This allows us to unload our bitterness and unforgiveness so that we can be completely free.

The Bible says bless those that curse you. If we can see the things that have come against us as a curse, then we also must realize that it is in our best interest to not only forgive, but also to bless the person who has offended us.

We will know we have forgiven when our feelings toward the other person have changed, and we are able to bless the person, even if their behaviors or actions are not what we would like to see.

Example prayer:

Lord, I take responsibility and repent for all the bitterness and unforgiveness in my life.

I am willing to give my end of the rope of unforgiveness to You, Lord, and allow You to take care of the situation for me.

Lord, I forgive everyone who has ever hurt me, misused me, mistreated me, abused me, abandoned me, rejected me, or who wasn't there for me when I needed them. It doesn't

Understanding Emotional Healing

mean what they did was right, it just means that I choose to trust You and give it to You, Lord, and I forgive them.

*Lord, Your Word says to bless[160] those that curse me, so I choose to bless **ALL** the people who have transgressed against me.*

And Lord, I forgive myself for every mistake that I have ever made, and I choose to receive the forgiveness that You have for me.

Lord, I ask that You would hold me in Your arms, protect me, love me, and heal me.

In Jesus Name, Amen.

Victim Mentality

When the Divine flow of God is interrupted, we may have a victim mentality that is blocking us from hearing the truth.

When the children of Israel came to the promised land, God told them to go take the promised land. So they sent spies to check out the land and the spies came back with an evil report and said there are giants in the land.

The spies declared that they were like grasshoppers[161] in their

---

[160] Matthew 5:44 But I say unto you, Love your enemies, bless them that curse you, do good to them that hate you, and pray for them which despitefully use you, and persecute you;

[161] Numbers 13:33 And there we saw the giants, the sons of Anak, which came of the giants: and we were in our

Blocks to Healing (S-Z)

own sight. With this report the people got discouraged and depressed.

God knew there was no way they were going to be able to fight the giants and win with a grasshopper mentality. So God changed his orders, and said do not go fight the giants.

When God changed his orders, they decided to go anyway. They got beaten badly because they disobeyed God when He told them not to go.

When we pray from the position of a victim, the more we pray the more depressed we get, because the prayers are connecting with the positive of God, and are revealing the victim mentality that we are praying from.

When we pray from a heavenly position, we will feel something rising up within us that causes us to see God in a bigger way, and our problems will get smaller and smaller.

When David came on the scene where Goliath was cursing the armies of God, everyone was scared of this big man, because they were comparing themselves to Goliath.

David could not understand why nobody was doing anything about this, because he was comparing the giant to God. It did not make sense to him that the people were afraid of the giant, because God is so much bigger than Goliath.

---

own sight as grasshoppers, and so we were in their sight.

Understanding Emotional Healing

David already saw the victory because he was connected to God, and he had no concept that the giant could win.

How many of our problems do we believe are bigger than God? The answer is **NONE OF OUR PROBLEMS ARE BIGGER THAN GOD.**

If we believe that none of our problems are bigger than God, then it is time that we start acting that way.

Example prayer:

Lord, I take responsibility and repent for not believing that You are big enough to handle my problems. Please remove all hopelessness, discouragement, and the victim mentality from my life, and help me to see the situation at hand from Your point of view.

Lord, I repent for allowing the victim spirit to operate in my life. I now choose to walk in the authority that You have given me, of being more than a conqueror[162].

In the name of Jesus, I command all depression to leave me right now.

Lord, I choose to believe in, and connect to, the power and authority that You have for me.

In Jesus Name, Amen.

---

[162] Romans 8:37-39 Nay, in all these things we are more than conquerors through him that loved us. For I am persuaded, that neither death, nor life, nor angels, nor principalities, nor powers, nor things present, nor things to come, nor height, nor depth, nor any other creature, shall be able to separate us from the love of God, which is in Christ Jesus our Lord.

Blocks to Healing (S-Z)

Vows, Oaths, and Agreements

Many times when people are having a hard time getting free, it can be helpful to check for vows, oaths, and/or agreements that are not in alignment with God.

For example, somebody might say "I will never be like my dad" or "When I grow up, I'm going to get even with them."

When a person declares that they do not want to be like their dad, etc. They are rejecting the good things about their dad and who God made their dad to be.

At the same time they are not discerning that the real enemy is not their dad, but the real enemy is the evil spirits that are working through their dad's insecurities.

With the declaration that we do not want to be like our dad, we block off who God made our dad to be, but instead we open up the generational evil spirits to work through us, that were attacking our dad.

These vows can keep us from having the ability to forgive. It blocks out the generational[163] blessings, and allows the bad things to come through anyway.

It is very important that we make our agreements with God, and break any and all agreements with the enemy.

---

[163] Deuteronomy 7:9 Know therefore that the LORD thy God, he is God, the faithful God, which keepeth covenant and mercy with them that love him and keep his commandments to a thousand generations;

Understanding Emotional Healing

Example prayer:

Lord, I take responsibility and repent for all the vows, oaths, and agreements that I have made that were not in alignment with You, and I ask that You would remove them from my life.

Lord, I now break any and all agreements with the enemy, and I choose to make my agreements with You from this day forward.

In Jesus Name, Amen.

Chapter 8: Keys to Overcoming

A small key can open a big door. In the same way, there are keys that we can use in the spirit realm to open and close doors so that our life can flow in the way God designed it to flow.

Keys also represent authority. If we have a key to a new car, we can drive that car. It is hard to push that car by hand. If we don't put the key into the ignition, and start the engine, the key is useless to us, and the car is useless to us.

In the following chapter we will speak about small keys that will open big doors and could very well be the thing that will unlock your freedom.

Acceptance

Many people have not been accepted for who they are, but they have been tolerated for what they can do. To effectively

Understanding Emotional Healing

help someone to be free, it works to start where people are, not where we want them to be.

If we can accept people beyond where they are accepting themselves, we can help them to get free. When people receive love and acceptance in areas where they have been used to being rejected, they get hooked by God.

When a fisherman is fishing and he hooks a fish, he is not hoping that the fish will swim straight to the boat. Part of the excitement for the fisherman is the struggle that the fish will display, while it is hooked, before it is landed in the boat.

God is not worried about people that put up a fight after they are hooked. When they buck and kick[164], it is not God who is getting hurt, it is themselves that are getting hurt.

There are many people who want to be free, but parts of them are more comfortable in their known misery, and they are not willing to take a chance on an unknown joy.

When a person has not received acceptance as a young child, or is not receiving acceptance in their life, they can very easily end up looking for love and acceptance in all the wrong places.

When we have unconditional love and acceptance for a person, it does not mean that we unconditionally accept every behavior or sin that the person is operating in. What it means is that we love and accept the person in spite of their conditions,

---

[164] acts 9:5 And he said, Who art thou, Lord? And the Lord said, I am Jesus whom thou persecutest: it is hard for thee to kick against the pricks.

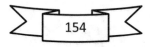

Keys to Overcoming

and then help them to change their behavior, and align their heart with God.

Authority

We have a lot more power and authority than we know.

Many people have been hurt by wrong authority, and hate any and all forms of authority. They have been programmed by the devil to hate authority.

Therefore, they throw away their God given authority. What they thought was authority wasn't actually true authority. It was someone misusing and abusing authority, because of their own insecurities.

If we can understand the difference between true and false authority we can begin to embrace the true authority and power.

If we throw away our authority we won't have access to it, and God doesn't have access to it either, because the devil picked it up when we rejected it.

Jesus took away the devil's authority at the cross. The only authority the devil has anymore is the authority that humans give him. If we reject our authority, the devil will begin to use it.

If we hate ourselves and reject ourselves, we are giving our authority to the enemy and he's using it against us.

We can step back into our authority by repenting to God, then our authority will be returned back to us.

Understanding Emotional Healing

Jesus will then make us sit together with Him in the Heavenly realm[165], in a position of authority. When we get moved into that position of authority in the Heavenly realm, and start praying from that position, our prayers will change.

From this position of authority, we are seated above our problems, and we will begin to look down on our problems, as we pray against fear, or whatever else is going on in our life.

If we are looking up at our problem, then we are not praying from a position of authority, but instead we are praying from the position of a victim.

When we receive Jesus as our Lord and Savior, we receive delegated authority immediately.   As we mature and walk in the fullness of who God wants us to be, we will experience many tests and trials.

As we pass the tests and trials, we earn authority based on overcoming the enemy of our past experiences. As we gain earned authority, we can move forward with power and eradicate the enemy from the places where he is squatting in our life.

There is an example in the Bible where people were trying to cast out demons. The demons said, Paul we know, and Jesus we know, but who are you[166]? The men did not have the authority to accomplish what they were attempting to do.

---

[165] Ephesians 2:6 And hath raised us up together, and made us sit together in heavenly places in Christ Jesus:

[166] acts 19:15 And the evil spirit answered and said, Jesus I know, and Paul I know; but who are ye?

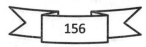

Keys to Overcoming

For example, if I start working at a business that is established and they have credit with another business, they could send me to pick up an order, and all I would have to do would be sign my name. I would be operating under their delegated authority.

If I start my own business, I would have to go through the process of establishing credit before I could just go pick up an order. This process is called earned authority.

In the same way, God allows us to go through certain processes and trials so that He can establish earned authority in us.

Forgiveness

Forgiveness is one of the most powerful tools that we have for freedom. When we forgive somebody, it is not saying that we agree with them, or that they did the right thing.

When we forgive, we are actually trusting God to take care of the problem. We are releasing ourselves from the responsibility of the situation, and we are giving it to God.

Forgiveness is like taking the rope of unforgiveness that is attached between ourselves and another person, disconnecting the rope from ourselves, and giving our end of the rope to God.

When we give our end of the rope to God, we are trusting Him to deal with the situation, and to deal with the other person. When we give God our end of the rope, He can start pulling on the other person, and start drawing them to Himself.

Understanding Emotional Healing

If we still want to get revenge[167] on the other person, or see them pay for it somehow, then it will be impossible for us to forgive them.

Unforgiveness is like being so mad at somebody that has wronged us, that we are willing to go to prison for them, because we hate them so much.

Forgiveness is like setting ourselves free from the prison that we put ourselves into when we got upset with the other person.

To experience true freedom, we need to forgive everyone who has ever hurt us, misused us, mistreated us, abused us, abandoned us, rejected us, or who wasn't there for us when we needed them.

To forgive somebody doesn't mean that we are saying what they did was right. It simply means that we choose to give it to God, and we forgive them.

It is also very important to forgive ourselves for every mistake that we ever made, and take those mistakes to the cross, and allow God to work them out for good[168].

Only by forgiving ourselves, can we receive the forgiveness that God has for us. He has already provided forgiveness for us, however, we cannot receive that forgiveness, if we do not forgive ourselves[169].

---

[167] Romans 12:19 Dearly beloved, avenge not yourselves, but rather give place unto wrath: for it is written, Vengeance is mine; I will repay, saith the Lord.

[168] Romans 8:28 And we know that all things work together for good to them that love God, to them who are the called according to his purpose.

[169] Mark 11:26 But if ye do not forgive, neither will your Father which is in Heaven forgive your trespasses.

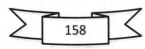

Keys to Overcoming

Grace

Grace is the power to do God's will when we are connected to God's spirit. It is not a license to do whatever we want to do in the flesh, and get away with it, and expect that God will just cover it without any consequences.

Why does it seem like the grace of God is not working in the church at this time? It is because God resists the proud[170], but gives grace to the humble.

The church can err on the side of preaching the grace message, without bringing into consideration that God might be resisting us, because of pride in our life.

If our hearts are full of pride, there is no wonder that some of these things are not working the way God designed them to work.

Some people are attempting to use grace as a license to do their own thing, thinking that they can have their own way now, and repent later. This is a mindset that people believe, that it is easier to ask for forgiveness, than to ask for permission.

For example, somebody said that they asked God for a bicycle. However, because they knew that God did not work that way, they stole a bicycle and then asked God to forgive them. This is not the way God designed it to work.

---

[170] James 4:6 But he giveth more grace. Wherefore he saith, God resisteth the proud, but giveth grace unto the humble.

Understanding Emotional Healing

Some people have accepted the false belief that, because Jesus died on the cross for us, and has paid for our sins, this somehow allows them to sin, or live in sin, and live irresponsibly without experiencing any consequences.

The enemy tricks them into believing that this is what grace is for. This is **DEFINITELY NOT** what grace is for.

One good picture to explain grace and faith is, grace is God extending His hand down to help us, while faith is us extending our hand up to God's hand of grace. True Godly power is released when the connection happens between grace and faith.

Gratefulness

The healthiest of all human emotions is gratitude. When we are grateful, we disable every single one of the enemy's plans.

When we are grateful for everything that happens in our life, it disables the enemy from working in our life, because of the power of gratitude.

God's plan is for us to be grateful in everything. He wants us to give thanks in all things[171]. He doesn't just want us to be grateful when things are going the way we want them to go. He wants us to be grateful even when it looks like the enemy is winning.

---

[171] Ephesians 5:20 Giving thanks always for all things unto God and the Father in the name of our Lord Jesus Christ;

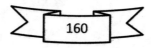

Keys to Overcoming

People use many different strategies in an effort to bury their past, and hide it behind walls of self-preservation in their heart. The problem with this is, Jesus came and died for our problems, our hurts, our past, our disappointments, and all the negative in our life.

When we bury our negative experiences and other issues of the past, these feelings that are buried alive will just stay under the surface, and will fester until something happens to trigger them.

When they get triggered, these buried negative feelings will pop up and take control of the person and the situation.

When we are grateful for our past, we do not allow these negative feelings to stay buried, but instead we become willing to face them, and surrender them to God.

When our past is surrendered to God, even when something comes up that needs to be dealt with, it does not have the ability to take control of us.

When we give our past to God, He will take our past and exchange it for true freedom.

Something shifted in our lives when we decided to thank God for every second of our past, turn our entire past over to God, and decided to completely trust Him with it.

When we trust God with our past, we know that He can make all things work together for good[172].

---

[172] Romans 8:28 And we know that all things work together for good to them that love God, to them who are the

Understanding Emotional Healing

When we are grateful for what Jesus did for us by dying on the cross for us, and we give everything to Him, we can be completely free in Him, and the enemy cannot get any foothold in our life.

Joy of the Lord

Joy is a position of authority over the issues and challenges of life. Joy is a free gift that is available through the exchange[173] that Jesus made available for us at the cross. It is a fruit of the Spirit.

There is a difference between joy and happiness. Joy is a gift from God that enables us to experience excitement in the midst of storms and trials. Happiness is a temporary feeling determined by our perception of the circumstances and issues we experience.

When things go our way, we can be very happy, but when things do not go our way, happiness leaves. Joy is much more deep-seated and permanent.

We can choose to submit to God and ask Him for His Divine joy to fill our hearts, deeper than every trauma, every hurt, every disappointment, etc.

The Bible says the joy of the Lord is our strength[174]. If we want some strength in our life, it is important that we start enjoying

---

called according to his purpose.

[173] Isaiah 61:3 To appoint unto them that mourn in Zion, to give unto them beauty for ashes, the oil of joy for mourning, the garment of praise for the spirit of heaviness; that they might be called trees of righteousness, the planting of the LORD, that he might be glorified.

[174] Nehemiah 8:10b ... for the joy of the LORD is your strength.

Keys to Overcoming

our life. Life is an interesting journey, and it can be enjoyable. Learn to enjoy the journey!

How can we enjoy the stuff that is coming against us? We can enjoy it when we know, and trust, that God is going to bring us through. He will give us keys to overcome the enemy.

After we get through something, God will often use us to help other people overcome their problems.

Peace that Passes Understanding

Peace is a free gift that is available by making Jesus Christ our Lord and Savior and by putting our full trust in Him.

When our full trust[175] is in the Lord, then no matter what storms and issues of life come against us, we can have peace because we know that it is in God's hands.

Peace is a fruit of the Spirit. It establishes a position of authority over the issues and challenges of life.

When we have the peace of God that passes all human understanding and reasoning, this peace will guard[176] our hearts and minds through Jesus Christ.

Peace is not something that we can create through compromise. Any attempts at accomplishing peace outside of the

---

[175] Proverbs 3:5 Trust in the LORD with all thine heart; and lean not unto thine own understanding.

[176] Philippians 4:7 And the peace of God, which passeth all understanding, shall keep your hearts and minds through Christ Jesus.

Understanding Emotional Healing

revelation of Jesus Christ, are nothing more than human efforts at fabricating a false and temporary peace.

This attempt of creating peace will only survive until our next disagreement.

True peace will not compromise the truth, but instead will be willing to face the things according to God's perspective.

Perfect Love Casts Out Fear

Are you ready for a more excellent way[177]? What is a more excellent way? Love is a more excellent way.

Love is expressed as an action and experienced as a feeling. It includes compassion, determination, tolerance, endurance, support, faith, and much more.

Love will open up the heart. When love comes into the heart, people will start to trust, and they are now ready to receive the truth. When people know the truth[178], the truth will make them free.

Truth doesn't open the heart, and love doesn't make us free. Love and truth together makes us free.

Love without truth is a compromise where anything, including sin, is tolerated.

---

[177] 1 Corinthians 12:31 But covet earnestly the best gifts: and yet shew I unto you a more excellent way.

[178] John 8:32 And ye shall know the truth, and the truth shall make you free.

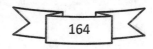

Keys to Overcoming

Truth without love is brutal, because without love the heart will not open. When the heart is not open, truth will demand obedience without question, and without relationship.

If we do all the right things, say all the right words, understand all the mysteries of life, have all knowledge, and have all kinds of faith, but do not use love, it means nothing[179].

If we give everything we have to feed the poor, and allow our body to be burned[180], but we don't have love, it doesn't help us at all. If we do not open our hearts to receive love from God, we are basically nothing.

Love suffers long and is kind, it does not envy, it does not behave rudely, it does not seek its own, and it thinks no evil. Love does not rejoice in iniquity, but it rejoices in truth. Love bears all things, believes all things, hopes all things, and endures all things.

When we are 'me' focused, it is not love, it is lust. Lust will honor ourselves at others' expense. True love will honor others at our expense. That is a good way to measure what we are doing, and why.

Love never fails.

---

[179] 1 Corinthians 13:2 And though I have the gift of prophecy, and understand all mysteries, and all knowledge; and though I have all faith, so that I could remove mountains, and have not charity, I am nothing.

[180] 1 Corinthians 13:3 And though I bestow all my goods to feed the poor, and though I give my body to be burned, and have not charity, it profiteth me nothing.

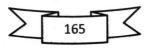

Understanding Emotional Healing

The Power of Our Words

The words that we speak are constantly creating who we are and creating the environment around us.

When we speak[181] words of life, it produces an atmosphere of life around us.

When we speak curses of death, it produces an atmosphere of depression and loneliness.

So let's take a good look at what we are saying. If we say, "I'm dying to get somewhere", could it be that we are actually speaking a curse of death over our body? Could it be that this gives cancer permission to start killing us?

What if some of our problems are coming from some of the things we are saying, and we don't even realize it because we have been tricked by the enemy, and deceived into saying these things which we never really mean?

What about this one? Someone says, "I was at the restaurant and it took forever until I got my food."

Why is this statement a problem? Because the Bible talks about what forever is. When we go to the restaurant and we say that it takes forever to get our food, and it was somewhere around 15 minutes, our brain will subconsciously automatically calculate that forever is somewhere around 15 minutes.

---

[181] Proverbs 18:21 Death and life are in the power of the tongue: and they that love it shall eat the fruit thereof.

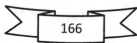

Keys to Overcoming

This new program then operates in other areas such as when we hear about hell being forever, our brain may calculate it to mean 15 minutes. This can subconsciously cause us to be desensitized to the consequences of sin.

This can happen on a subconscious level that most people are not even aware of.

Let's start speaking life and truth into our situations. Let's start speaking life and truth to each other. Let's start speaking life and truth to the people around us, instead of tearing down and criticizing them.

Let's make a conscious effort to watch what the words are that are coming out of our mouth. Are these words speaking life, or are they speaking curses over ourselves or others?

The Power of Submission

Submission means plugging into a power source, for example, submitting an extension cord into a receptacle in the wall. If there is power in the receptacle, we will have full power at the other end of the cord.

We have just as much power at the other end of the cord as we have when we plug directly into the wall. However, the cord has absolutely no power if it is not submitted into the receptacle.

When we submit[182] to God, we will have power to resist the enemy, and the enemy will flee. Jesus was submitted to God and

---

[182] James 4:7 Submit yourselves therefore to God. Resist the devil, and he will flee from you.

Understanding Emotional Healing

told his disciples that He only does[183] what He sees the Father doing.

When a man is submitted to Christ, God will give him a vision for his family. By submitting to that vision, he can lead with the full power and authority that God intended for his family.

When a wife submits to her husband[184], and the vision that God gave him, she can plug into the power and authority that God intended for her to have.

It does not mean she becomes a doormat for somebody else's insecurities. It means that she can plug into God's original plan and purpose for her life, and the life of her family.

When God gives a person a vision[185], the vision is the final authority. God will then set up leaders of the vision.

As long as the leaders connect with, and stay submitted to, the vision, God will bring others into the vision to participate, benefit, and help to advance the vision.

When people submit to the vision, their gifts are activated, and the whole community begins to flow together, as one, to fulfill a greater purpose.

---

[183] John 5:19 Then answered Jesus and said unto them, Verily, verily, I say unto you, The Son can do nothing of himself, but what he seeth the Father do: for what things soever he doeth, these also doeth to the Son likewise.
[184] Ephesians 5:23 For the husband is the head of the wife, even as Christ is the head of the church: and he is the saviour of the body.
[185] Proverbs 29:18 Where there is no vision, the people perish: but he that keepeth the law, happy is he.

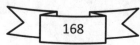

Keys to Overcoming

Submitting ourselves one to another[186] simply means we are coming into agreement with the power of God working through each other, and the purposes that God has put into each others' lives. It does not mean that some insecure dictator can now do whatever he wants to.

If we stay in the spirit, and stay submitted to God, we can pray against whatever comes against the vision, and the enemy has to leave because we are submitted to the vision. If we get offended, it allows the enemy to disrupt and destroy the vision.

If we bring a situation into the natural realm, then the person with the most physical strength wins.

If we keep the situation in the spirit realm[187], the person with the most spiritual authority wins. Only by connecting to God's vision can a person have spiritual authority.

The Power of the Trash Can

Do we all have a trashcan in our house? Why do we have a trashcan? Why don't we just take the trash out and not worry about having a trashcan? It is because **TRASH HAPPENS!**

As we go through life, trash will continue to happen, and things will happen where people will not always agree with what we're doing.

---

[186] Ephesians 5:21 Submitting yourselves one to another in the fear of God.

[187] Ephesians 6:12 For we wrestle not against flesh and blood, but against principalities, against powers, against the rulers of the darkness of this world, against spiritual wickedness in high places.

Understanding Emotional Healing

People won't always approve of us, rejection will come against us, fear will come at us, and many other things can happen. Can we remember to put these things into the trashcan?

If we can remember this, we can put our daily things into the trashcan, and when the trashcan is full, we can take it to the dumpster. How do we take it to the dumpster in the spirit? We talk to God, and we give Him the trash, and we leave it there.

When we put things into the trashcan, it is trash. It is not a good idea to compare trash. We don't need to analyze, is it clean trash, is it dirty trash, is it big trash, is it small trash.

If the devil says anything, put it in the trashcan. If the devil quotes Scriptures, put it in the trashcan, because the devil quotes Scriptures out of context.

Many people are walking around with clutter in their lives. They don't want to get rid of their stuff because they might need it in 10 years from now.

The problem with not getting rid of clutter is, it will bog us down and keep us from moving forward as fast. Every time we need to find something, we need to dig around for a while before we can find it. Usually we will go and buy a new one, because it's easier than digging around the clutter looking for it.

There are many people walking around with spiritual clutter in their lives. This clutter is holding back many people from moving on to the fullness of what God has prepared for them.

Keys to Overcoming

If we are holding onto mindsets and experiences that are outdated and half worn out, we can be standing in the way of what God is doing next.

Let's remember to take the trash and the clutter and put it in the trash can, take it to God, and leave it with Him.

The Shelf

Many people try to make decisions by figuring out if something is yes or no. The problem with this is, many situations in life have dynamics which we don't understand.

When we don't understand something, and we only have a yes or no option, it forces us to say no to anything that is new or that we don't understand.

There is a better way. We can build a shelf in our life, in the spirit realm, where we can put situations, questions, experiences, and other things, until we get more clarity. After we receive clarity, we can move it to the 'yes' or the 'no' option.

If we only have a 'yes' and a 'no' option, it is impossible for us to enjoy eating a chicken leg. The proper way to eat a chicken leg is to eat the meat and throw away the bone.

However, if it is either 'yes' or 'no', then we would either have to eat the whole thing, bones and all, or not eat any of it, because it has bones in it. It is much better to eat the meat, and throw away the bones.

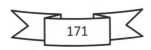

Understanding Emotional Healing

In the same way, when we have the shelf option for our life, it gives us the ability to hear what people are saying, even if we don't agree with everything that they are saying.

Whatever parts we agree with them, we can put on the 'yes' option. Whatever we don't agree with them, we can put on the 'no' option.

Whatever we don't know or understand yet, we can put on the shelf for further discernment.

Using the shelf is an ongoing process of putting things on the shelf, and taking them off of the shelf.

For instance, some of the things that we had in the 'yes' option for a number of years, we may later find out that it needs further discernment because of some new information that we found out.

At this point we can take it from the 'yes' option and put it on the shelf for further discernment.

The Truth Will Make Us Free

Truth is the truth according to what God says. We cannot make the truth be what we want it to be. We are only free when we allow God's view of truth to make us free.

Some versions of the Bible say the truth will <u>set</u> us free. Some versions of the Bible say the truth will <u>make</u> us free.

Keys to Overcoming

A number of years ago, I had a vision of the difference between the truth setting us free, and the truth making us free. In this vision, I saw a bird flying around in a cage.

Someone came and opened the door of the cage, and set the bird free. The bird continued to fly around in the cage saying, "I am free, I am free." As the bird continued to fly around in the cage, I saw a hand reach into the cage, and take the bird out of the cage, and **make** it free.

Some people believe that they cannot be free until others around them are free. If we are dependent on the others getting freedom, before we can move forward in life, it will cause us to judge the other people, and to blame them for us not being able to get free.

Love will open up the heart. When love comes into the heart, people will start to trust, and they are now ready to receive the truth. When people know the truth[188], the truth will make them free.

Truth doesn't open the heart, and love doesn't make us free. Love and truth together makes us free.

Love without truth is a compromise where anything, including sin, is tolerated.

Truth without love is brutal, because without love the heart will not open. When the heart is not open, truth will demand obedience without question, and without relationship.

---

[188] John 8:32 And ye shall know the truth, and the truth shall make you free.

Understanding Emotional Healing

Chapter 9: Steps to Overcoming

Every situation in our life has the potential to be a stumbling block or a stepping stone. We make the choice to either stumble over the challenges of life, or to step up onto them. We can only step up unto them by trusting God, and allowing Him to direct our path[189].

It can be very helpful in our life, if we understand some of the steps that we can take to overcome the challenges of life.

These steps can be like climbing a ladder. If we miss a step, it can be very difficult, or even impossible, to move forward in life.

---

[189] Proverbs 3:5-6 Trust in the LORD with all thine heart; and lean not unto thine own understanding. In all thy ways acknowledge him, and he shall direct thy paths.

Understanding Emotional Healing

Repentance and Salvation

True repentance comes from a love for God, and a sincere desire to obey His commandments. It is when a person makes a radical turn from one way of life to another.

True repentance is a summons to a personal, absolute, and unconditional surrender to God as sovereign in our life. It requires taking on a whole new point of view, and looking at things God's way.

True repentance is a change of the mind and the heart, that brings a fresh attitude toward God, oneself, and life in general. Repentance implies that a person turns away from evil, and turns his heart and will to God, submitting to God's commandments. It means to totally and completely forsake sin.

When we repent to God, and surrender our life to Him, we can receive forgiveness for our sins, through the blood of Jesus, that was shed for us at the cross at Calvary.

When we become born again, we are now born from above, instead of living from below in the flesh. Because of being born from above, we are now in Christ and we become a new creature[190].

Our spirit gets instantly brand new when we become born-again. However, our soul has to go through a transformation[191] process, and sanctification[192] through the

---

[190] 2 Corinthians 5:17 Therefore if any man be in Christ, he is a new creature: old things are passed away; behold, all things are become new.

[191] Romans 12:2 And be not conformed to this world: but be ye transformed by the renewing of your mind, that

Steps to Overcoming

truth, for us to be able to operate, and function, the way God designed for us to function.

So in reality what happens is, our spirit is brand-new, but our soul still has issues. Our soul needs to be transformed by the renewing of our mind, and our body will prosper, and be in health, even as our soul prospers[193].

For us to flow with God, through the Holy Spirit, our spirit needs to be in charge of our soul, and our physical body. We then can surrender our spirit to the Holy Spirit, which allows us to live and function in the power of God.

For us to manifest the spirit of God here on earth, our soul has to be in alignment with the spirit, so that we can manifest the spiritual realm realities on a physical level.

We are to manifest the character of God in the physical realm. The things of the spirit cannot be naturally discerned[194], because the natural person cannot see the things of the spirit.

For us to make a difference to the people around us, we have to manifest in the natural, the things that we receive in the spirit. We can only do this by aligning the spirit, the soul, and the body in Divine order.

---

ye may prove what is that good, and acceptable, and perfect, will of God.

[192] John 17:19 And for their sakes I sanctify myself, that they also might be sanctified through the truth.

[193] 3 John 1:2 Beloved, I wish above all things that thou mayest prosper and be in health, even as thy soul prospereth.

[194] 1 Corinthians 2:14 But the natural man receiveth not the things of the Spirit of God: for they are foolishness unto him: neither can he know them, because they are spiritually discerned.

Understanding Emotional Healing

Activating Our Will and Taking Responsibility

Many people have passively laid down their will, or have had events happen in their life that broke their will.

For us to find freedom, it is necessary for us to take responsibility for our life, which means to pick up our will where we had left it, or where it was damaged or broken.

When we take responsibility for our life, we stand in the authority that we have in Christ, and we do something about our situation.

Only after picking up our will, and repenting for the areas where we have misused our will, can we surrender our will to God.

When we fully surrender our will to God, it is no longer us that are living, but it is now Christ[195] that is living in us.

Imagine that you go to a fast food restaurant, and you order a sandwich and french fries. After you have driven away and you check your bag, you notice there are only a few french fries in your bag. You may get upset that you did not get what you paid for.

The question to ask ourselves is this, when Jesus died on the cross for me, did He get what He paid for? Am I being all that He created me to be?

---

[195] Galatians 2:20 I am crucified with Christ: nevertheless I live; yet not I, but Christ liveth in me: and the life which I now live in the flesh I live by the faith of the Son of God, who loved me, and gave himself for me.

Steps to Overcoming

God needs two things from us. He needs our willingness and obedience. If we are willing and obedient, God can take us where He wants us to go.

Closing Doors

Many times when people are not experiencing healing, it can be because of an open door in their life in the spirit realm.

If this is not fully understood, we may be trying to receive healing, without dealing with the issues that were allowing the sickness to occur in the first place.

If we don't deal with the real reason that this sickness occurred, we may only be dealing with the symptoms instead of removing the root that caused the open door in the first place.

When we only focus on the symptoms, to deal with the problem it is like having a low oil light coming on in a vehicle, and instead of adding oil, we cut the wire to the low oil light.

It is better to find out why we have the symptoms, and to deal with the root causes, than to focus on managing the symptoms.

If we do not deal with the root cause of the issue, it is like taking a weed-eater and trimming the weeds, instead of pulling the weeds out by the roots.

If we only trim the weeds, they will grow back very quickly. If we pull them out by the roots, it completely removes them, and they will not grow again.

Understanding Emotional Healing

If we would come home, and the neighbor's dog was in our house, what would we do? Would we not chase it out? What would we do if it came back in? Would it not make sense to look for open doors where the dog was coming in?

Many people have allowed the enemy to build strongholds in their lives. These strongholds are allowing open doors for the enemy to have continued access to their lives.

These strongholds may even include generational strongholds that were passed down from the generations before them. These open doors are allowing the enemy to work and cause havoc in people's lives.

We can experience true freedom when we take responsibility and repent for any and all open doors, and ask God to close the doors and cleanse us from all unrighteousness.

Taking Every Thought Captive

Many of life's problems are caused by the thoughts that we think. The enemy is constantly bombarding us with negative thoughts, tempting thoughts, and destructive thoughts.

This can even include thoughts that seem positive such as, telling us how good we are at something that we do, in an attempt to get us to stumble because of pride.

We can even have thoughts of fear that will come against us, attack us, and try to disable us. When fear first comes to us, it comes in the form of a thought.

Steps to Overcoming

The Bible talks about taking **every** thought captive[196], and bringing it to the obedience of Christ. It is helpful to see ourselves as a policeman who is handcuffing the thoughts, and bringing them to Jesus.

Can we visualize that? Can we see ourselves running after the thoughts, jumping on them, wrestling them down, and handcuffing them? After they are handcuffed, can we visualize taking the handcuffed thoughts and bringing them to Jesus?

Many people try to pray against the thoughts, push the thoughts away, dodge the thoughts, or hide from them. This never works for them, because it is not the way God designed it to work. God designed it for us to take the thoughts captive.

If we do not take the thoughts captive, they will take us captive and control us.

Feelings are caused by the perception of what we believe, which comes from what we think and believe. When we take our thoughts captive, it will also change the way we feel.

Feelings Buried Alive Never Die

People use many different strategies in an effort to bury their past, and hide it behind walls of self-preservation in their heart.

The problem with this is, Jesus came and died for our

---

[196] 2 Corinthians 10:5 Casting down imaginations, and every high thing that exalteth itself against the knowledge of God, and bringing into captivity every thought to the obedience of Christ;

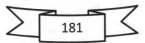

Understanding Emotional Healing

problems, our hurts, our past, our disappointments, and all the negative in our life.

When we bury our negative experiences and other issues of the past, these feelings that are buried alive will just stay under the surface, and will fester until something happens to trigger them.

When they get triggered, these buried negative feelings will pop up and take control of the person and the situation.

When we are grateful for our past, we do not allow these negative feelings to stay buried, but instead we become willing to face them, and surrender them to God.

When our past is surrendered to God, even when something comes up that needs to be dealt with, it does not have the ability to take control of us.

When we give our past to God, He will take our past and exchange it for true freedom.

Turn On the Light

Light will always expel darkness. Darkness can never cast out light.

If somebody has a gun pointed at me, they cannot pull that trigger unless they have fear. If I have perfect love they can't access their fear to pull the trigger, because perfect love casts out fear.

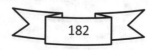

Steps to Overcoming

Fear does not cast out perfect love, and darkness never ever casts out light.

When you are in your home, you can curse the darkness all night, and command it to leave in the name of Jesus, and it won't happen. Or you can just flip on the light switch and the darkness will leave immediately.

There are too many people trying to cast out demons, instead of just turning on the light. When the light comes in, the darkness leaves immediately.

We are not saying we never cast out demons. What we are saying is, when the light comes into the person, there is no more room for darkness.

Jesus said that we are the light[197] of the world. He tells us to let our light shine[198]. How are we doing with letting our light shine?

Trading

When we join God's Kingdom, we have an opportunity to bring all our problems, our trash, our hurts, and everything from our past, to God through the cross[199].

---

[197] Matthew 5:14 Ye are the light of the world. A city that is set on an hill cannot be hid.

[198] Matthew 5:16 Let your light so shine before men, that they may see your good works, and glorify your Father which is in heaven.

[199] 2 Corinthians 5:21 For he hath made him to be sin for us, who knew no sin; that we might be made the righteousness of God in him.

Understanding Emotional Healing

When we bring these things to Him, God will trade[200] our trash for His treasures. He tells us that He will give us beauty for ashes, oil of Joy for our mourning, and the garment of praise for the spirit of heaviness. Wow! What a trade!

It is very important for us to remember, that in order to trade-in our trash, we must let go of the trash that we were holding on to, so that the trade can be completed, and we can receive the treasures that God has for us.

When we bring our past to God, the things that happened in our past will now work together for good[201].

Healing Vs. Divine Health

We can be healed over and over and over again, but God's perfect will is not to heal us. God's perfect will is that we live in Divine health[202], and not get sick in the first place.

For example, if we receive physical healing, but we continue to eat at fast food restaurants every single day, we can expect to reap the consequences of our poor choices.

Another example is, if we have a cluttered up car, and we decide one day to clean it up,   that would be like a healing. Even

---

[200] Isaiah 61:3 To appoint unto them that mourn in Zion, to give unto them beauty for ashes, the oil of joy for mourning, the garment of praise for the spirit of heaviness; that they might be called trees of righteousness, the planting of the LORD, that he might be glorified.

[201] Romans 8:28 And we know that all things work together for good to them that love God, to them who are the called according to his purpose.

[202] 3 John 1:2 Beloved, I wish above all things that thou mayest prosper and be in health, even as thy soul prospereth.

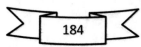

Steps to Overcoming

though the car is clean, if we do not change our habits, it will not take long for the car to be cluttered up again.

When we change our habits, and clean up after ourselves, we can experience Divine health.

Unity in Diversity

Unity[203] in diversity is when we flow together with one[204] heart, one faith, one baptism, one body, and one Lord, even though there are different callings, cultures, and opinions. The word university comes from unity in diversity.

The Bible talks about the members[205] of the body[206] all flowing together. God might have a different purpose for different denominations, cultures, and people groups, but they need to be open, and flow together with each other and with God.

In our physical body the common denominator is the blood. The blood touches all the organs, muscles, tissues, and cells.

The common denominator in the body of Christ is the blood of Jesus. We cut ourselves off from the flow of God, when we

---

[203] Ephesians 4:3 Endeavouring to keep the unity of the Spirit in the bond of peace.

[204] Ephesians 4:4-6 There is one body, and one Spirit, even as ye are called in one hope of your calling; One Lord, one faith, one baptism, One God and Father of all, who is above all, and through all, and in you all.

[205] 1 Corinthians 12:14 For the body is not one member, but many.

[206] 1 Corinthians 12:20 But now are they many members, yet but one body.

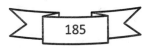

Understanding Emotional Healing

compare[207] ourselves one to another, and decide if we are better or worse than the other person.

If we compare ourselves, then we need to come up with an answer on whether we are superior or inferior. When we look to Jesus, then we can compare it to what Jesus says, and we don't have to worry about comparing it to other people.

If everybody looks to Jesus, we can all come together in unity, in the spirit realm, in Jesus. Then we can all flow together and quit trying to control and change each other.

For example, if I move my arm, two different muscles in my arm may need to move in two opposite directions, in order to work together.

It is possible for God to tell one person to pull, and another person to release, in the same day, and they both heard God. If we get stuck on, "I heard this", "you heard that", so one of us must not be hearing from God, then we may be completely missing what God is developing in our lives.

God might have two people hearing completely opposite things and they could both be right.

If we have strongholds we need to hammer through, one person may hear God say, "Hit it hard", and another person may hear God say "Retreat". That can flow together if we understand what God is doing.

---

[207] 2 Corinthians 10:12 For we dare not make ourselves of the number, or compare ourselves with some that commend themselves: but they measuring themselves by themselves, and comparing themselves among themselves, are not wise.

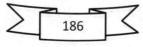

Steps to Overcoming

However, if we argue about it, we might both miss the point. If we can expand our mind, so that we can see the bigger picture, from God's perspective, we can be free.

Laying Up Treasures in Heaven

When we look over our life, we can determine how much of it was focused on laying up treasures[208] in earth, and how much is focused on laying up treasures in Heaven.

When we lay up treasures in earth, we are focusing on self and self protection. When we lay up treasures in Heaven, we are focused on helping others, being grateful to God, and advancing the Kingdom of God.

When we spend money, we either spend it on ourselves, or we spend it on advancing God's Kingdom.

When we focus on the earth realm, we look at the dollar as the currency that we value things to. When we focus on the spirit realm, we focus on favor, influence, and faith, as the currency of Heaven.

Are we focusing on spending our talents to advance ourselves, or are we focusing on investing our talents to advance God's Kingdom?

---

[208] Matthew 6:19-21 Lay not up for yourselves treasures upon earth, where moth and rust doth corrupt, and where thieves break through and steal: But lay up for yourselves treasures in heaven, where neither moth nor rust doth corrupt, and where thieves do not break through nor steal: For where your treasure is, there will your heart be also.

Understanding Emotional Healing

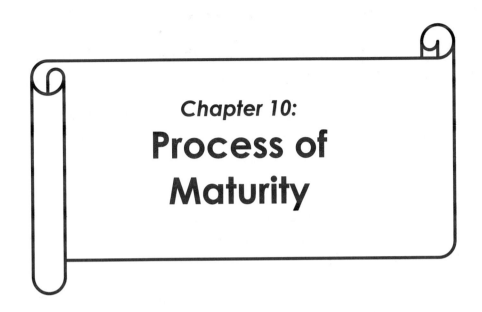

Chapter 10: Process of Maturity

There is a process to maturity, which will lead us to the fullness of who we are in Christ.

When we were a little child, our parents did everything for us. As we grew up, we started doing things for ourselves. Later in life we started doing things for others.

When we got married, we took responsibility for doing things for our spouse and children. As the children grew, we took responsibility to teach them how to live for God, for themselves, and for others.

As we walk through life, we study things that are in our own maturity level, and we only know that we are advancing, when we see that we are passing the tests. As we pass the tests and move forward in the next levels of maturity, we can now safely move forward with more responsibility, and be a blessing to others.

Understanding Emotional Healing

When the children of Israel took over the promised land, God told them that he will only give them the land little by little[209].

If He would have given them all the land at once, they could not have occupied it. The land would have become desolate, and the beasts of the field would have taken it over again.

There is a principle of taking back ground from the enemy, and there is a principle of occupying, and keeping what we took back. If we do not occupy, or keep what we took back, the enemy will claim it again.

When the disciples started walking with Jesus, Jesus did the work and the disciples watched. As the disciples matured, Jesus did the work, and the disciples helped. Later on, the disciples were sent out, and Jesus helped them. Finally, the disciples did the work and Jesus left.

Memories

Memories do not hold us in bondage. Our past does not hold us in bondage. It is our perception of the memories, and the perception of the past, that holds us in bondage.

Our perception is what we believe about something that happened. When we believe that what happened in our life was all bad, it is always, always, always because of believing that God was not in control, or that God somehow got this one wrong, and 'I' have to step in and do something about it.

---

[209] Exodus 23:29-30 I will not drive them out from before thee in one year; lest the land become desolate, and the beast of the field multiply against thee. By little and little I will drive them out from before thee, until thou be increased, and inherit the land.

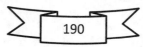

Process of Maturity

These mindsets can get programmed into us at a young age[210], and then these patterns continue to work in us, even as adults, if these lies are not dealt with and replaced with truth.

If we do not base our life on the word of God and God's truth, then we will continue to react out of the patterns of lies.

If we continue to believe the lies we will get triggered, and in those triggers we will operate from our default system that was programmed into us by those lies.

There are many people living in adult bodies, but inside of themselves, they are living and acting like children. The reason for this may be that things have happened when they were small, and they got stuck there because of lies or trauma.

It is like we have a CD player and we hit the pause button. It will just sit there and spin, not moving forward, until we hit the play button again.

When things happened to us as a small child, we may not have understood what was happening, and therefore believed the lies. These lies will then hold us in bondage until we replace them with the truth.

When we embrace the Truth, we can begin to know the Truth, which means to have an intimate relationship with the Truth. When we know the Truth, the Truth will make us free[211].

---

[210] 1 Corinthians 13:11 When I was a child, I spake as a child, I understood as a child, I thought as a child: but when I became a man, I put away childish things.

[211] John 8:32 And ye shall know the truth, and the truth shall make you free.

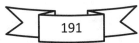

Understanding Emotional Healing

Triggers

When we get triggered, we flip back into our old default system, and we act out of that system that might have been installed when we were only a few years old.

Now, as adults, we might still be going back to the default system that was operating in us at a very young age.

When I was a child, I spoke as a child, I understood as a child, I thought as a child. But when I became a man, I put away childish things[212]. This means that I now have a new default system, and I can now do what God wants me to do.

If we understand how this works, and can change our default program, then we can start responding to people and situations, instead of reacting to them.

If we react, we allow some demonic influence to take over for awhile, (maybe only for a short period of time), because we don't trust God.

If we recognize the reaction, and what is happening, then we can repent and bring it to the light, and receive healing from God.

The key is to bring it to the light, because Jesus did not die for the garbage that we bury. He died for the things that we reveal. So if we can bring it to the light the darkness leaves.

---

[212] 1 Corinthians 13:11 When I was a child, I spake as a child, I understood as a child, I thought as a child: but when I became a man, I put away childish things.

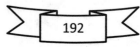

Process of Maturity

We bring it to the light by confessing[213] our faults one to another, and praying one for another.

If we keep things hidden it means that we don't trust God to heal it, and we are still trying to deal with it ourselves. If we bring it to the light, God will take it and heal it.

Weaning

As we mature in God's Kingdom, God will begin to remove our dependency from man, in order to turn it unto Him.

If a baby is not being weaned, is it the baby's fault, or is it the mother's fault? Is it not the mother's responsibility to wean the child?

In the church today it seems like many people want to continue to breast-feed as baby Christians, instead of maturing into God's plan for their life.

Many people are stuck because they refuse to be weaned, and move on with God. It is time to move beyond breast-feeding. It is time to move beyond the milk.

There is a special grace for baby Christians to act up and act goofy. However, when it comes time to wean and they still act like a baby, it becomes obnoxious.

---

[213] James 5:16 Confess your faults one to another, and pray one for another, that ye may be healed. The effectual fervent prayer of a righteous man availeth much.

Understanding Emotional Healing

As time goes on we pick up more responsibility. We will begin to mature and take on a more active role in advancing God's Kingdom.

If we give our children a chore such as washing the dishes, we don't just say to them, "Go wash the dishes." We first take them through a training process and teach them how to wash the dishes.

The time will come when we can say to them, "Go wash the dishes." At that time we don't want them asking if they should wash the plates first, if they should wash the cups first, or if they should wash the spoons first.

Because of the training, they already know what washing the dishes means.

The time comes when we might say, "For the next whole week, every day at lunch time, it is your job to do the dishes."

We don't want them asking every day if they have to do the dishes again today, because we had already given them the assignment, in the beginning of the week, that they are on duty for the whole week.

Later the time will come when it is their regular job, and they do it without being told.

There are certain things God expects us to do, whether He's telling us to do them or not, because He has already trained us that way.

Process of Maturity

Jesus said, "I do nothing of myself; but as my Father taught[214] me."

We know that to help people, pleases God. We don't have to hear God to know if we should be kind to people or help people. We don't have to hear God to know if we should be respectful today.

There are things that we can do because we know that's how God does it. We can do it because that's what we see the Father doing.

If we are waiting on God, and God is waiting on us, we have a problem.

Maturity

There is a process to maturity, and as we grow and mature, we start taking responsibility for more and more things.

We believe there are people in the body of Christ that God is training to do certain missions and assignments. When He says, "Go do it," they will know exactly what He means, without needing the details every single time.

A lot of Christians won't obey God because God didn't give them specific details. He gave them a command but instead of obeying immediately, they are waiting on God for the details that they already know.

---

[214] John 8:28b ... and that I do nothing of myself; but as my Father hath taught me, I speak these things.

Understanding Emotional Healing

While they are waiting on God, He is waiting on them to obey His commands. They know what the next steps are to do, and they have been trained how to do it, but because they don't see **all** the steps, they refuse to get started.

If we are at a traffic light in town, and the light is green, do we wait to go until all the other lights are green? No, we go through the light that is green, and if we get to a red light, we stop.

In the same way, when God gives us a green light, we go. If we come to a red light, we stop and wait until it turns green.

Another example is, when we have a young child, we will not give them the keys to a car. There are certain maturity levels and certain tests that need to be passed in order for someone to get a driver's license.

If a father gives a young child the keys to a car, and the child has a car wreck, whose fault is it? Would it not be the father's fault, because he gave the child the keys before he was responsible enough to handle the responsibility of the job?

We believe there are many Christians who would love to have responsibility in the Kingdom of God, but they have not reached certain maturity levels and have not passed certain tests[215] that are needed in order for God to trust them to do those very things.

---

[215] Galatians 4:1-5 Now I say, That the heir, as long as he is a child, differeth nothing from a servant, though he be lord of all; But is under tutors and Governors until the time appointed of the father. Even so we, when we were children, were in bondage under the elements of the world: But when the fullness of the time was come, God sent forth his Son, made of a woman, made under the law, To redeem them that were under the law, that we might receive the adoption of sons.

Process of Maturity

If we want to have more responsibility in the Kingdom of God, we need to be willing to be weaned of our old mindsets and comfort levels. We need to quit whining and complaining when things don't go our way, and instead make a decision to trust God.

Discipleship

A disciple is one who embraces, and assists in spreading the teachings of another. It is a person who is a pupil, supporter, or follower of the doctrines or beliefs of another.

Jesus seemed to think discipleship was a big deal, putting it as the heart of the great commission, to teach all nations[216].

Jesus was always consistent in His relationship to God. A Christian must be consistent in his relationship to the life of Jesus in him.

Many Christians are compromising their relationship with God, to strict unyielding doctrines lacking the power of God.

Many people pour themselves into their own doctrines, and God has to blast them out of their preconceived ideas, before they can become devoted to Jesus Christ.

True discipleship is to be more like Jesus, where Christ-like transformation is the goal, by putting on the mind of Christ.

---

[216] Matthew 28:19-20 Go ye therefore, and teach all nations, baptizing them in the name of the Father, and of the Son, and of the Holy Ghost: Teaching them to observe all things whatsoever I have commanded you: and, lo, I am with you alway, even unto the end of the world. Amen.

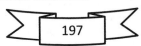

Understanding Emotional Healing

The point of discipleship is not about information, but of Christ-like transformation. That means it is not about knowledge in general, but about knowing Jesus better.

Trying to be like Jesus, without the power of Jesus, dishonors Jesus.

In the Bible we can find four levels of discipleship.
- First, Jesus called them to be disciples, and they watched Him as He did the work.
- Second, Jesus did the work, and the disciples helped[217] Him.
- Third, the disciples did the work, and Jesus worked with[218] them.
- Fourth, Jesus left[219], and the disciples did the work.

Sonship

The Bible calls us to be sons[220] of God. In the Jewish culture, to be a son meant that the father would put the son in a position of authority.

If we have a business, and put somebody in charge of a certain division of that business, we don't want him calling us for every little detail.

---

[217] Matthew 14:19 And he commanded the multitude to sit down on the grass, and took the five loaves, and the two fishes, and looking up to Heaven, he blessed, and brake, and gave the loaves to his disciples, and the disciples to the multitude.
[218] Mark 16:20 And they went forth, and preached every where, the Lord working with them, and confirming the word with signs following. Amen.
[219] Acts 1:9 And when he had spoken these things, while they beheld, he was taken up; and a cloud received him out of their sight.
[220] Romans 8:14 For as many as are led by the Spirit of God, they are the sons of God.

Process of Maturity

We put him in charge to take care of the details. His job is to get the materials that are needed and do what he was trained to do.

There's an element of delegation that God wants to do, where he puts us in charge of certain situations, and we do them without needing to ask about every detail.

I was in charge of a division at a company where I was not the owner, but I was the manager of that division. If the owner walked into the shop, he would ask me how things were going.

However, since he had made me the manager of the division, if he came into the shop, he did not automatically take over, because he had given me the authority to run the shop.

In the beginning, God gave Adam and Eve the power, and authority, to have dominion on earth, and to subdue[221] it.

The devil tricked them out of their dominion. Jesus bought it back by dying on the cross and paying for the curse. Jesus then gave the authority back to us.

We now have the opportunity to be ambassadors[222] for Christ here on earth, and bring alignment to earth, through our prayers and obedience.

---

[221] Genesis 1:28 And God blessed them, and God said unto them, Be fruitful, and multiply, and replenish the earth, and subdue it: and have dominion over the fish of the sea, and over the fowl of the air, and over every living thing that moveth upon the earth.

[222] 2 Corinthians 5:20 Now then we are ambassadors for Christ, as though God did beseech you by us: we pray you in Christ's stead, be ye reconciled to God.

Understanding Emotional Healing

Community

We know in part, and we prophesy in part[223]. That is the reason why it so important to work together, because we all have a part.

If we understand that, we can bring our parts together and see an even bigger picture, where everyone can move forward in greater power and victory, as a community, in God's kingdom.

The enemy tries to get us to believe that we have all the answers, and everybody else should do things our way. If we are not careful we can get into the thought pattern that we have it all together and other people are wrong.

When we realize that everyone has had their own experiences, and we all have the opportunity to put our experiences together, then we can see an even greater picture the way God sees things.

When we all come together and we focus on finding the heart of God in the matter, we will all get a bigger picture as a community.

For a community to prosper, it is important to empower everyone in their God-given callings.

---

[223] 1 Corinthians 13:9-10 For we know in part, and we prophesy in part. But when that which is perfect is come, then that which is in part shall be done away.

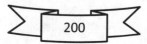

Process of Maturity

Body of Christ

In the physical body, every part of the body gets their commands from the head. There are many different organs, tissues, and muscles. There are trillions of cells, and every cell gets it's command from the head.

There is a certain DNA in every cell, that tells each specific cell what to do and be.

Every organ in our body is formed by a cluster of cells that are obedient to the DNA commands that God gave them.

As the spiritual body, which is the body of Christ[224], every person gets their command from the Head[225], which is Jesus Christ.

There are many different ministries, churches, functions, and groups, and they all get their commands from the Head.

The different ministries and churches, in the body of Christ, are groups of people that are obedient to the commands that God is giving them, to do specific projects.

When the people in the body of Christ are disobedient to their instructions from the Head, Jesus Christ, we call this spiritual cancer.

---

[224] 1 Corinthians 12:12 For as the body is one, and hath many members, and all the members of that one body, being many, are one body: so also is Christ.

[225] Ephesians 4:15 But speaking the truth in love, may grow up into him in all things, which is the head, even Christ:

Understanding Emotional Healing

In our opinion, the body of Christ has a form of cancer, but we believe it will be healed. If we can see the truth and what is actually happening, we will be able to come into alignment with what God is doing.

Chapter 11: How to Help People with Emotional Issues

If we want to help people with emotional issues, we really need to care about them as a person. They will be able to detect if we really care about them or if we just want to fix them.

When they are talking, they will be checking to see if we are listening with our heart. They want to know if we really care about their heart. Does our heart care about their heart?

When a hurting person is testing the listener, they are not trying to make it difficult for the sake of being difficult. They are trying to determine if the listener has the capacity to handle the hurt.

When we are helping a hurting person, we may need to pass some tests. These tests will be in the specific area where others have hurt them.

Understanding Emotional Healing

To really know what a person is actually saying we need to listen very intently. We need to make sure we hear what they are really saying. We also need to know what they are trying to say that they are not saying.

Many times people are not quite saying what they are trying to say. They may be trying to say something behind what they are saying. It often helps to repeat back to them what you think you heard them say, and ask them if that is what they are trying to say.

In order to effectively help people, it is important to meet them where they are and not where you want them to be.

The Position and Process

There is a difference in the position and the process. The position is a state of being, according to God's design. The process is coming into alignment and agreement with who we already are.

As we walk through life, we either believe that we are an overcomer, or we believe that we are a victim. It depends on which position we believe we are in. We will process according to what we believe, and our life will manifest what we believe.

Many people are declaring that they are standing on a position. However, they are having difficulty to know how to walk out the process of the declaration that they are standing on.

Other people are focusing on the process. However, they may not understand that it is important to first stand on the position.

How to Help People with Emotional Issues

When a princess is born, she is a princess the day she is born. She may cry at night, need to be fed, or need her diaper changed, but she is still a princess.

Later on she might roll in the mud, but she is still a princess. As she grows up, she may need some training to learn how to be the princess that she already is.

In the same way, a child of God may need some training to learn how to be the Christian that they already are.

The Power of Asking Questions

Many people have been told all their lives how to live, what to do, etc. They may not even have been taught how to think for themselves, or how to pick up their own will.

Asking questions gets people to talk. When they hear themselves talk, many times they will hear their own answers.

Asking questions gets people to think for themselves, and then they learn. It also helps to draw out the person's heart.

When a person's heart opens up, whatever is in the heart will begin to come forth.

There are many different types of questions such as:
- Safe questions
- Closed questions
- Reflective questions
- Open questions

Understanding Emotional Healing

- Hypothetical questions
- Interview questions
- Harmonious questions

Safe questions will relax and draw out the other person. Safe questions are easy to answer. They are effortless, which makes the person feel comfortable. Responses to safe questions do not require deep thought.

Examples of safe questions would be:
- How's the weather?
- Isn't this a beautiful day?

Closed questions are like true or false, yes or no, or multiple-choice requests of one or two word responses. Closed questions are valuable for obtaining specific facts. If closed questions are used too much, people may feel as if they are being interrogated.

Suggested beginnings for closed questions would be:
- Are you willing...
- Do you want...

Reflective questions are used to reflect back what you think a person meant by what they said. It can check if you really understand what they are saying. This is useful in dealing with angry or difficult people. Reflective questions are very useful in conflict situations.

Suggested beginnings for reflective questions would be:
- So are you saying...
- So is this what I'm hearing you say...

How to Help People with Emotional Issues

Open questions are more like essay questions. They allow the individual to elaborate. Open questions cause a person to continue to share because of the interest that they sense coming from you.

Open questions will uncover a person's passion. It discovers what makes a person come to life.

Suggested beginnings for open questions would be:
- What do you love about...
- How do you feel about...
- In what way do you think this will...
- What is your biggest challenge in life...

Sometimes they are statements such as:
- Tell me about...
- Give me an example of...

Hypothetical questions open a person's imagination to the future. This can be very helpful if a person has lost hope. Hypothetical questions can cause a person to think of a similar situation. They also can be used to find out how the person would do with a new situation.

Hypothetical questions are used to win the battle ahead of time, so that when a situation arises, the person already has overcome the difficulty in the spirit realm.

Suggested beginnings for hypothetical questions would be:
- What would you do if...
- How would you cope with...
- How would you deal with...

Understanding Emotional Healing

Interview questions zero in on a particular area. They are more in depth and allow you to get closer to the person. Interview questions cause values to emerge and they are more intellectual than feeling.

Suggested beginnings for interview questions would be:
- What do you think about...
- How do you feel about...

Listen to what the person is saying and form an interview question using the person's words. For example, if a person uses the word icky, do not change it to yucky, when you ask your next question.

Harmonious questions involve the feelings and bring about harmony between you and the other person. They will cause deep self-disclosure. Harmonious questions are on target, sensitive, and get to the core value of the person.

Harmonious questions usually will reveal the core belief system, and expose the lies, that are keeping the person in bondage.

Suggested beginnings for harmonious questions would be:
- When did you decide to...
- What would need to exist in order for...
- So when this happened, how did you feel about...

The Ability to Listen

Many people struggle with emotional baggage because they feel like they have never been heard. If we have the ability to

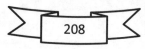

How to Help People with Emotional Issues

listen to them they will suddenly feel like they have been heard. This will help them to be willing to take an honest look at their own heart.

To really hear a person's heart, we have to stay present to them in the moment. It does not work to listen half-heartedly, and be distracted at the same time.

The ability to listen means first of all to really hear what the person is saying. It also means to hear what the person is saying that they are not saying. What do they mean by what they say or don't say?

When we are listening to somebody, it is important that we do not jump ahead of them, to where we think they are going. If we try to jump to where we think they are going, we may completely miss what they are trying to say.

It is also important to not interrupt the person when they are trying to verbalize or communicate a thought. When we interrupt a person to try to help them say what we think they are trying to say, they may go with what we are saying instead of what they were starting to say.

However that may not be what they were trying to bring out. It may be easier for them to agree with what they think we were trying to say, than to actually say what they were going to say.

If a person is struggling with trying to put into words what they are feeling, do not rescue them by providing words for them.

Understanding Emotional Healing

If we rescue them when they are trying to express themselves, it can hinder the process and keep us from hearing their heart.

When we truly listen to what they are saying we may be able to hear some key information that will bring clarity to their situation.

Changing Our Perceptions

If we are on an escalator, and the escalator stops, does that mean that we are stuck?

If the escalator stops, we can stand there defeated, waiting for somebody to come to rescue us. Or we can take the next step and walk right out of our situation. We are only stuck if we believe the escalator is responsible to get us all the way to the top or bottom.

The reason we get stuck in our life is because we are focusing on our own inability, instead of focusing on God's ability to bring us through our problems.

It is our perception that keeps us stuck. Our perception is what we believe about something that happened in our life, which may or may not be the truth.

For example, if we were hurt when we were in third grade in school, and now years later we remember it, the pain that we feel actually comes from the perception of the memory, not from the memory itself. The perception that we have determines the emotions that we feel.

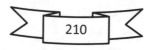

How to Help People with Emotional Issues

Here is an example of how quickly our perceptions can be changed.

A man was working late on a Friday night. He came home from a business meeting about 3 o'clock in the morning, and was planning to sleep in on Saturday morning, because he had nothing planned for the day.

For an ongoing period of time before this, his children had the habit of screaming while they were playing. He had been working with them to play quietly instead of screaming.

He woke up early on Saturday morning to the screams of his child. At this point he is very upset. He gets out of bed, goes into the kitchen where the screams are coming from, ready to bring the rod of correction on this child.

As he enters the kitchen, he sees his child with a hand stuck in the door. How long do you think it took his feelings to change? Even though nothing changed other than his perception, his feelings changed instantly.

Nothing changed in his environment except his perception of what was going on, but immediately he changed from anger to compassion.

When we change our perception, we can go from begging and pleading with God to do things for us, to seeing ourselves seated[226] with Christ in the Heavenly realm, far above our problems.

---

[226] Ephesians 2:6 And hath raised us up together, and made us sit together in heavenly places in Christ Jesus:

Understanding Emotional Healing

We can then speak to the problems from our position of authority, and command the problems to bow to the plans and purposes of God.

Counseling Sessions vs. Relationships

Many people who are helping others with emotional issues will find themselves in a struggle. The struggle is understanding the difference between relationships and counseling sessions.

If we don't understand the difference between relationships and counseling sessions it can go either way.

The people that are hurting can violate relationships by demanding individual time, from a person who has a heart to help, when they are in a relational setting.

The person who has a heart to help can damage the relationship by turning a relational moment into a counseling session.

Counseling deals with issues and situations while relationships deal with the people themselves. It is important to have specific times for counseling, and also to have separate times for relationships.

The key to overcoming this struggle is to recognize the difference between the people and their issues.

Chapter 12: Aligning the Spirit, Soul, and Body

When we repent to God, and surrender our life to Him, we can receive forgiveness for our sins, through the blood of Jesus, that was shed for us on the cross at Calvary.

When we become born again, we are now born from above, instead of living from below in the flesh. Because of being born from above, we are now in Christ and we become a new creature[227].

Our spirit is instantly brand new when we get born-again. However, our soul has to go through a transformation[228] process, and sanctification[229] through the truth, for us to be able

---

[227] 2 Corinthians 5:17 Therefore if any man be in Christ, he is a new creature: old things are passed away; behold, all things are become new.

[228] Romans 12:2 And be not conformed to this world: but be ye transformed by the renewing of your mind, that ye may prove what is that good, and acceptable, and perfect, will of God.

[229] John 17:19 And for their sakes I sanctify myself, that they also might be sanctified through the truth.

Understanding Emotional Healing

to operate, and function, the way God designed for us to function.

So in reality what happens is, our spirit is brand-new, but our soul still has issues. Our soul needs to be transformed by the renewing of our mind, and our body will prosper and be in health, even as our soul prospers[230].

For us to flow with God, through the Holy Spirit, our spirit needs to be in charge of our soul, and our physical body. We then can surrender our spirit to the Holy Spirit, which allows us to live and function in the power of God.

For us to manifest the spirit of God here on earth, our soul has to be in alignment with the spirit, so that we can manifest the spiritual realm realities on a physical level.

We are to manifest the character of God in the physical realm. The things of the spirit cannot be naturally discerned[231], because the natural person cannot see the things of the spirit.

For us to make a difference to the people around us, we have to manifest in the natural, the things that we receive in the spirit. We can only do this by aligning the spirit, the soul, and the body in Divine order.

As we surrender to God, He will show us the issues that we need to deal with.

---

[230] 3 John 1:2 Beloved, I wish above all things that thou mayest prosper and be in health, even as thy soul prospereth.
[231] 1 Corinthians 2:14 But the natural man receiveth not the things of the Spirit of God: for they are foolishness unto him: neither can he know them, because they are spiritually discerned.

Aligning the Spirit, Soul, and Body

Feeding the Spirit, Soul, and Body

We are a three-part being. We are a spirit, a soul, and a physical body. Actually we could say, "I am a spirit, I have a soul, and I live in this motorhome." (physical body)

The spirit is who we actually are, and we live in the physical body. The soul is our communication system between the spirit and the physical.

If we would compare it to an airplane, we would say that our spirit is the pilot, our soul is the instrument panels and the communication equipment, and our physical body would be the actual aircraft.

Each part of our being feeds in a different way. Our physical body feeds on the food that we eat. The physical well-being of our body is affected by the quality of food that we eat.

If we just eat junk food, it will affect our physical being. It is much better for us to eat quality food and watch what we eat for our physical well-being.

What does our spirit feed on? Our spirit is fed when we get a revelation. Many people believe that our spirit is fed by the Word of God, which is not completely false.

However, when we read the Word of God, and do not get a revelation of the Word, we do not get fed by the Word until it becomes a revelation to us. This does not mean that we should not read the Word of God, but instead it means that we ask God to make his Word a revelation to us.

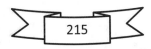

Understanding Emotional Healing

Many times we may read God's Word, and later it becomes revelation to us. At the time that it becomes revelation to us, is when we got fed with that revelation.

It is still beneficial to read God's Word, and to store it inside of us until such a time that it becomes revelation to us.

It is also possible for us to get revelation in other ways in which God is speaking to us. It is very important that the revelation is actually coming from God and is not a deception that can hinder our spiritual growth.

What does our soul feed on? Our soul is fed when we receive acceptance. Ultimately it is best for us to receive this acceptance from God.

However, it is also important for us to be able to accept each other, and to be there for each other, and to pray for each other. The other area that we need acceptance from, is to accept ourselves the way God made us, instead of rejecting who we are.

Imagine this, a couple who had not been to church for a while, decided to go to church on a Sunday morning. They walk into the church and sat into somebody else's pew, they didn't have the right clothes on, they didn't say the right words, they didn't worship correctly, and they were not very churchy.

Everybody in church was acting snobbish and disrespectful to them, because they don't fit into the mold that the church was used to operating in.

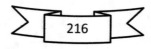

Aligning the Spirit, Soul, and Body

After church they decided to stop in at the local bar where they knew their friends were hanging out. As they walked into the bar, they got welcomed in and were made to feel right at home.

Where did their soul get fed? Is it possible that the bars are doing a better job of feeding people's souls than the churches are? What would happen if the Christians would do a better job of accepting people the way they are, and then helping them to freedom?

Connecting to the Source

When we are using a computer, we can either download a bunch of information onto the computer, which slows down the computer, or we can access it through the Internet and the information never gets downloaded onto the computer.

If we are connected to the Internet, the information is still available, but it does not bog down the computer.

In the same way, we can connect to God through the Holy Spirit and get the information that we need without overloading our mind with trying to figure everything out.

If our heart is shut down, we cannot access what God wants us to hear.

If we have a need to be in control, we will have a need to figure everything out, and our mind will overload with information, which slows us down so that we cannot walk in the fullness that God has for us.

Understanding Emotional Healing

A man went to the dentist, and after the dentist was finished, the man said, "Thank God".

The dentist then told the man that he does not believe in God. If there is a God, why is evil running rampant and bad stuff is happening to people? Why is there so much pain and suffering on this earth if there is a God?

The man then told the dentist, in that case he doesn't believe in dentists. If there are dentists, why do people have decayed teeth, capped teeth, broken teeth, toothaches, and gum problems?

The dentist said it is because they don't make the choice to come to him for help.

In the same way, instead of blaming God for the problems, we have an opportunity to come to Him for the solution. However, it is our choice. We need to make a decision and choose to allow God to take care of our problems.

Being an Overcomer

We need to understand Truth and Godly principles, and apply them to our lives, so we can have the power to overcome.

There are a lot of people that are trying to overcome in a wrong way. If you look at the Biblical principles of overcoming, it is not shouting louder, it is not praying longer, and it is not reading the Bible more.

Aligning the Spirit, Soul, and Body

We want to clarify that we are not against shouting louder, we are not against reading the Bible more, and we are not against praying more.

There will be times for that, but if we do not apply the Biblical Truth according to God and His Kingdom, we can shout and perform until we are hoarse and discouraged.

We can read the Bible day and night, and we can pray with everything we've got, and we will get very little results unless we connect to God.

As a demonstration, try to drive a vehicle without starting the engine. Get into the vehicle but don't turn the key on. Put your hands on the steering wheel, make all kinds of engine sounds, stomp the accelerator and the brakes, and try to turn the steering wheel.

You can pretend that you're going somewhere, and if that doesn't work, just make some louder noises, and get yourself pumped up more, and things like that.

This is what it looks like when people try to get God's attention without being willing to do it God's way.

God gives us the keys and truths, not just to pretend to have power, but to actually start this thing up and experience the power to overcome.

As a little child, I would pretend I was driving the tractor. When I grew up, I started actually driving the tractor. I found out

Understanding Emotional Healing

there is a big difference in pretending to drive a tractor or to actually drive it.

There is also a **big difference** in pretending that we are doing the will of God, and actually doing the will of God.

There is a big difference when we apply God's principles and watch them work in our life, versus pretending to do the will of God, and not getting the desired results.

When we fully connect to God, and we are willing to live our life God's way, then we will have the power to be an overcomer. We will then be used by God to overcome the plans of the enemy and to destroy the enemy's kingdom.

Using the Owner's Manual

Many people believe that reading the Bible is a **duty** that is required by God. They believe they need to read the Bible to please God.

They think God is in Heaven watching to make sure that they read enough chapters per day, or spend enough time per day in reading His Word.

An owner's manual is designed to communicate to the buyer how to use a specific product to the fullest potential. Many people have tools and gadgets they use on a regular basis.

However, because they have not fully read and understood the owner's manual, they use less than 25% of the functions that are available for their use.

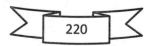

Aligning the Spirit, Soul, and Body

The Bible is actually our owner's manual. It explains the way we were designed to operate and function. It is to our benefit to understand the principles and plans of God's design for mankind.

When we understand God's plans and purposes, we can operate in the power and authority that God created for us to operate in.

When we read the Bible we will begin to understand:
- The benefits that we have
- The authority that we have as ambassadors in God's kingdom
- The pitfalls to avoid
- The advantages that we have
- The secrets to living
- The blessings of aligning with God
- The curses of aligning with the devil
- The power that is available to God's people
- The keys of how to have access to the awesome truth and love of God.

When we begin to understand the plans that God has for mankind, our hearts and our minds will be opened to the amazing revelation of the unfair advantage that we have over the enemy's Kingdom.

The Bible tells us how to operate in God's Kingdom and how to advance God's Kingdom.

Understanding Emotional Healing

Additional Resources and Opportunities

Understanding Emotional Healing

'Overcomers Course'

The 'Overcomers Course' is a 5 day group healing, teaching, training and development course. It is designed to help individuals and couples to overcome obstacles in their life, and find the freedom and the flow of God's order for their life.

For more information and testimonies about the 'Overcomers Course' call or go to:

www.overcomerscourse.com

or click on the 'Overcomers Course' page on our website.

Additional Resources and Opportunities

Thank - you!

We trust you enjoyed reading this book and found it to be a valuable tool.

We appreciate any feedback that you may have about this project.

If you have a testimony about how this book impacted your life, and would be willing to allow us to use it on (either or all, of the following areas of advertising:) website, social media, e-blast, or newsletter. We would love to hear from you.

If you have a Testimony and do not want us to use it in advertising we still want to hear from you. Specify whether we are allowed to use it or not.

You can either write it out and mail it to us, email it to us, or video record your testimony.

Please keep us in prayer as we seek to advance the Kingdom of God here on earth.

God bless you,
Impact Media Publishing, LLC
P.O. Box 567
Ephrata, PA 17522

sales@impactmediapublishing.com
www.lappbrothers.com 717-859-2614

Understanding Emotional Healing

This book was written for the individual reader as well as for group study.

It is available to use for small group study in your home or church.

If you are blessed by this book, please go to: www.amazon.com and leave a review for us!
Go to: www.amazon.com, search for "Understanding Emotional Healing", go about halfway down the webpage and click on Write Customer review.
Your review could help take this book to the top of the charts on Amazon.com

Together we can help more people be blessed and experience true freedom!